EMBODIED
CLERGY WOMEN AND
THE SOLIDARITY OF A MOTHERING GOD

EMBODIED
CLERGY WOMEN AND
THE SOLIDARITY OF A MOTHERING GOD

LEE ANN M. POMRENKE

CHURCH
PUBLISHING
INCORPORATED

Church Publishing
19 East 34th Street
New York, NY 10016
www.churchpublishing.org

Cover design by Paul Soupiset
Typeset by Rose Design

A record of this book is available from the Library of Congress.

ISBN-13: 978-1-64065-309-2 (paperback)
ISBN-13: 978-1-64065-310-8 (ebook)

For Stefan, Vikta, and Greta

CONTENTS

INTRODUCTION

Solidarity

"You did that good deed of adopting a child, and now God is rewarding you with one of your own!"

I blinked at the church lady. There were so many things to address, I did not know where to start. I went for human agency, with a gritted-teeth smile. "This pregnancy was not a surprise. We chose to adopt first, then to try making her a sibling."

I also could have dived into theology: Is God really that involved with whether we conceive? We say that children are a blessing, but does that mean that people who cannot conceive are not blessed, or have not pleased God in some way? What about the fifty percent of pregnancies that are unintended—some conceived in violence, some of which cause great hardship for the mothers— how is God feeling about them? For heaven's sake, do you think I waited for or value our first child any less than the one I will birth? By the way, you do not say things like this to other families at our church or in the neighborhood, do you? I had so many topics to handle, but in the handshaking line at the end of a church service, practicality won.

In the moment I assumed that the fact-checking answer had a slightly higher chance of changing the story the church member was telling, than the faith-related questions. Yet there are bound to be opportunities to dig into all these thoughts in my life as a clergy mother. Incidents like the brief conversation above are opportunities not just to explain my personal actions, but to challenge all of our assumptions in healthy ways. Being a pastor and a mom makes me and my family obvious case studies for many topics related to

God and families (since we are already front and center and being discussed anyway). Sometimes the issues are practical, but frequently they beg for solid theological wrestling.

Certainly people talked about male clergy's families before women were commonly seen in pastoral leadership. Yet somehow the PKs of male pastors did not reflect to the same degree on their father as they do on a mother, and the church's historical use of mostly father images for God and male clergy for centuries enabled us to skirt the edges of these conversations. Now that clergy mothers are here in numbers, one of our many gifts to the church is instigating conversations by simply existing, such as:

- What is church for, in the lives of families with children, teens, and young adults? Why do we want them to experience belonging in church, and how do we pursue that?

- Do we expect or allow our clergy to give their personal relationships as much attention as they need? Is the model of professional ministry we have been operating with healthy for everyone?

- How does God really relate to us? Is it only as we associate culturally with fatherhood, or also the intimate, mutual impact of mothering?

We are all having bits of these conversations on the fly, but with close reading of the Bible and clergy mothers' experiences mixed in, this book is designed to spark deeper understanding within our congregations, including more frequent recognition of God's mothering activities among us and the experiences of solidarity that recognition can offer. What is the point of solidarity? It is significant to feel "seen," to know that others understand your experience, so they can fully empathize. Yet solidarity is even more than a feeling of togetherness. It is community that empowers us not only to keep going and survive, but with each other's determination and collected wisdom, to build power together. To stand in solidarity at a protest is to show with our bodies that we are neither small nor insignificant. To show up physically, acknowledging how people behave around our bodies, is a testimony to how people treat the image of God reflected in us. To show up with our voices and our stories is a testimony to God's ongoing, loving actions standing with those of us in need of mothering, and those doing the mothering.

This is not a book for clergy mothers alone. We do not need to rehearse these stories among ourselves or discover God's mothering actions in isolation. We need our congregations to learn from and with us, to explore these similarities between our ministries and God's mothering behaviors and to develop a shared commitment to act upon them together. Otherwise, nothing will change. A clergy mother reading this book may feel a kinship with others who name her experiences, but she will still be carrying her experiences alone. By reading and discussing this book together with congregation members, clergy mothers and congregation members can decide together how to work on our family system and to sustain the leadership of clergy mothers. This is a true support system.

Together, we become a force advocating for a better life. Commiseration will only get us so far. God's commiserating with us through becoming human in Jesus is meaningful, but it does not stop there. God not only feels what we feel through Jesus, but by sharing God's own similar experiences alongside ours, gives us new ways to live into resurrection and redemption even here, even now. That is why this is not a biography, although clergy mother stories abound. *Embodied* is about finding the echoes of our own stories in God's story, the solidarity that leads to new life out of death. Preachers, this is what we do. Congregation members, this is what we hope you do with us.

My experience is limited, as a white mother in predominantly white mainline Protestant churches. Some experiences of mothering are common to many, as are many of the expectations and tasks of being a pastor. Although I can read, talk with, and learn from others, I do not embody, so cannot fully comprehend, the experience of being a mother of color in the United States today. Neither can I know fully the experience of women who lead in Evangelical or Pentecostal congregations, with cultural dynamics I have never navigated. I only show up in my own body, but in the actions we have in common, we can testify to God's solidarity together.

I am keenly aware that I would not be a clergy mother, nor would I see God reflected in those identities, without the legacy of the women who blazed this path before me. My ordination was neither exceptional nor controversial because of the ordinations of women in my denomination fifty years ago and in all the years since. I recognize a mothering God theology in the lives of clergy women because of feminist and womanist theologians, who began pushing the limits of academic theology before I was born. I start with the assumption that women have voices that matter and contribute to everyone's understanding of the relationship between God and humanity because feminist theologians like Rosemary Ruether and Delores Williams stretched the limits of interpretation to include our perspectives. These same theologians might criticize my associating the intimate, nurturing behaviors of God with a gendered role, because tending relationships should be the domain of every Christian. I believe we can get there by giving credit to women for intimate caregiving and naming it mothering, while promising that these actions could be exercised by anybody. May later generations recognize the mothering actions of God reflected in us and assume that is a theology upon which they can build.

A Note on Word Choice and Metaphor

Throughout this book I will use "mother" as shorthand for an intimately involved, emotionally invested caregiver, and "mothering" for the nurturing actions we count on the central figure in our family to provide. That is not to say that fathers or gender non-binary parents do not behave in these ways, especially those who are the primary caregivers for their children. Indeed, they may be "mothering" in many ways every day. In a 2016 survey, the Pew Research Center reported that today's fathers in the U.S. spend three times as much time caregiving for their kids than they reported in 1965. It is still significantly less than mothers but headed in the right direction. However, as many times as the metaphor of Father God is repeated throughout the world, we can stand to honor and pay theological attention to what has, and overwhelmingly still is, women's work.

God does not have a gender, yet for centuries Christians chose the pronouns *he/him/his* to describe God. During the same many years, "mankind" was used as the inclusive term for all of humankind, or "men" was supposed to mean "all people." Meanwhile there was very little theological reflection on mothering. God still does not have a gender, but while discussing actions that have a gendered association such as mothering, we might reclaim a little bit of time and theological reflection with the pronouns *she/her/hers* for God as they seem to fit. Although co-parenting fathers, single fathers, and stay-at-home fathers perform mothering actions, we do not have to name those specific actions after them for them to be included. When it is not overly awkward to do so, I have replaced pronouns with the name of God to remind us of God's nongendered being. The language we use for God always influences our understanding and the authority we associate with certain voices in the church. I hope the words for God and God's behaviors described in the following pages lift up women's leadership, not only as equally important to that of men, but as unique and worthy of attention and value.

We also must acknowledge that not all mothers do these actions described as mothering, caring for their children fiercely and consistently. Mothers fail their children for all kinds of reasons, including systemic oppression, personal trauma, and addiction. A mothering God may not sound any safer or more loving than Father God does to those who experienced abusive or neglectful parents. Again, we are looking more at the actions we strive for as mothers.

Any human metaphor for God breaks down at some point, as God is so much more than human, and is far beyond our human understanding. I am interpreting God's behaviors and *perhaps* underlying emotional experiences in light of my own, as a testimony from motherhood and the life of a clergy woman. When I bear witness to how I recognize God's action in the world echoed in clergy mothers' experiences, I testify to how even I am made in God's image. I hope to inspire others to see God's solidarity in their own experiences.

In comparing the role of mother to the role of pastor, I draw some parallels between children in a household and members in a congregation. Of course this is not analogous, as many church members are adults with various skills and traits that steer the congregation and provide care for each other. The analogy does not need to be taken as condescending. We are all children compared to God. To be led, cared for, and taught like children can describe the caregiver's actions of great love, not superiority. That is my intention. Children change their parents as much as we influence them, and so it is in between clergy and the members in the pews. Bristling at this comparison I think says more about how we value children in our families than anything else. To God, we are all cherished children.

CHAPTER 1

The Wait

Never in my life have I waited more than I do on these children. Even to become a parent, the waiting was excruciating. My spouse and I waited through missteps and heart-wrenching decisions for our adoption placement, then for months to be able to have our daughter in our arms. Our older daughter was herself in the category of "waiting children," waiting to leave the children's home in Eastern Europe where she had lived all of her two years up until that point. We were all waiting for things none of us knew, like how becoming a family can help us all to heal and thrive, but also rip our hearts wide open and strain every relationship because the losses out of which our family emerged will never go away. We waited to bond solidly with our first child before we tried to conceive a younger sibling. While our second child grew in my uterus, my mother stayed with us for a month because the doctor thought I would deliver early (although I ended up going five days past the due date) asking frequently, "Well, do you feel anything? Wouldn't today be a good day to go into labor?" And our congregation waited with us. Well, sort of.

The congregation I served as pastor during both our adoption and pregnancy was in on our news, but only once it was relatively certain. They did not know all of our struggles in the process, on purpose. They did not know that the referral call with our first daughter's profile came while our congregation hosted a conference for ALLIA, All Liberian Lutherans In the Americas. They did not know I was hiding nausea and extreme fatigue during the first trimester of pregnancy. Even when I did share our reasons and decisions related to becoming parents, congregation members listened and interpreted them according to their own biases.

Our church was supportive, as best they knew how. They love children, and it was so touching the way that the other children enveloped our toddler with hands to hold and buddies to sit with as soon as she came home to our family. But during the Wait, comments like "It will all happen in God's time" made me cringe and hear anew how unhelpful such platitudes are for those waiting to become parents. My anxiety over wanting her with us immediately was exacerbated by my physician husband framing his own frustration through developmental milestones: "Between ages two and three are crucial months for brain development. We have to get her here and connected with resources ASAP!" Yet I knew that many West African members of our congregation had left children behind with extended family for years, since their visas only included certain family members. Month- or year-long separations were the norm for them. Was my "wait" so much more heartbreaking than theirs?

Demonstrating fertility and birthing children are so valued in that same immigrant community that adoption as my husband and I were pursuing it was a strange concept to our church members from West Africa. I overheard well-meaning church people talking about me, honestly wondering why we would adopt "someone else's child" unless I could not birth one of my own. There were cultural assumptions in there for sure, but that bias is also pretty common among white Americans. Even the judge in Eastern Europe questioned us on this during our court proceedings to adopt. Back home, the congregation waited with us, but only in part as I was too emotionally exhausted to sort out any misconceptions with them.

Most congregants feel they know the pastor, but much of the time, congregations only see what priests and pastors choose to show them. The pre-parenting stage is one of those times when women clergy especially will choose to be circumspect. The uncertainty of adoption added more layers in my case. I appreciated people wanting to celebrate with us but felt like that was only half of the story. Any adoption is preceded by a profound loss for the child and brings unknown challenges ahead for the entire family. Some adoptive parents are also grieving their own fertility struggles. There is a deep tangle of emotions behind our news of becoming parents. Keeping our adoption process quiet until it was certain was also a practical decision for me. If people are too empathetic or kind to me, I start tearing up. I could function better in my work, instead of dissolving into a puddle, if nobody knew the fears and desperate hopes occupying my mind most of the time.

During the wait for our second child, as I became visibly pregnant, our older daughter developed some new attachment issues. Viktoria was two-and-a-half years old when she joined our family through adoption and had never shown any separation anxiety when attending preschool or other group activities. She had cheerfully waved goodbye and gone back to playing. But now, at almost four, our Vikta had to be carried out of the sanctuary sobbing if she could not be near me. It is very challenging to deliver the words of institution or distribute communion with a child attached to one's leg. I would try to lead her to the back of the sanctuary during the sharing of the peace, so my husband could quickly get her out the door before she became distinctly not peaceful as the liturgy continued. The wait for her younger sister changed how we all felt about and approached our family participating in church. If there was a reason I could think of—a meeting after worship, or confirmation classes all afternoon—we would all breathe a sigh of relief that my husband and daughter should stay at home instead of commuting across town with me for the unpredictable ordeal. Congregation members asked about our daughter and missed seeing her, but I could not function as a pastor otherwise. Had I been more confident in blending my mom and pastor identities, or in the congregation's ability to embrace or support those two fully on display together, I might have handled that phase differently. Maybe I would have seen the opportunity to preach about God as mother and embody it. But at the time I was simply attempting to survive the painful phase. In her limited vocabulary for many months afterward, even once I was officially "on leave from call" and we were worshiping at a new church, Vikta summarized: "Me cry old church. Wanna be with Mama whole time." I remember, baby, and it was almost more than I could stand.

Becoming a mother told every other mother how vulnerable I had become. My heart is walking around in the world with my children and I would do anything for the love of them. Mothers can embody the meaning of "to lay down one's life" for another (John 15:13). That makes me incredibly vulnerable. I never put into words publicly how much the process of becoming Viktoria's mother pulled apart my heart or hers and put them back together again in a new formation, but other mothers can guess. The closest question people asked about my transformation was, "How are you adjusting?" to which my answer had to be, "immediately."

Just as congregations have a limited perspective on the pastor's family planning, Christians have little to go on when we wonder about God's motivations for relating to us as a parent. We only see now as if in a mirror dimly, as 1 Corinthians 13 puts it, and admittedly through our own biases. Why did God want to nurture children in God's own image? Do any parent's intentions end up matching reality anyway? Christians can speculate among ourselves, but we only have God's actions described in Genesis or the Gospels, not the emotional backstory. Why—in our creation stories—does God choose to parent older human beings first (Adam and Eve), instead of making newborns, who are so much more easily influenced and molded? Why does God choose to "adopt" Abraham, then create Jesus by birth?

Waiting seems to be key to becoming parents and prepares us for this identity. What if planting the tree of the knowledge of good and evil in the midst of the garden was not designed to test Adam and Eve's faithfulness? What if it was done so that God could wait, then mother the two through their mistakes? God and human beings could thereby become family. The children's defiance can be assumed in the plot of humankind (we know what we are like). But through presenting a choice, in the form of a tree bearing tantalizing fruit, the creator-creature relationship turned into a parent-child relationship. This relationship is even more fundamental to our identity and faith than the original sin. The pattern of every biblical story from then on becomes thus: we think we know better, but God will never stop loving us through every failure. God will be there, as a mother who cannot let us suffer without experiencing great agony herself, to pick up our pieces. God waited for her children to act independently, giving them the means to make the choice, but preparing them to make the right one. If we are going to see the time in Eden as any kind of test, perhaps it is one of God, mothering for the first time. God becomes a mother when she has to abandon parenting by decree and adjust to loving children through the consequences of their defiant actions. God no longer operates on the premise "Let there be . . . and it was so" because loving parents know that is never the end of the story.

What is a mothering God's first step following the admission of Adam and Eve's guilt? She makes them clothes herself. God knows the human beings are ashamed; that is the natural consequence of having their eyes opened to what they have done. Yet God does not dismiss their actions. There are consequences, and God will let them live with them. God takes her time and demonstrates loving care to meet their new needs, created by their defiance. The act of sewing clothes for Adam and Eve is what mothers do. We make a way for our children to move forward, even when they do not deserve it, creating an opportunity to learn to recover from their failures, not simply to follow directions blindly. This loving nurture is even more potent when done with our own hands (sewing those clothes ourselves). I would stitch these words onto my children if I could: "I forgive you. You are not to be ashamed. You are my child." From this point forward, God's entire story contained in the Bible is defined by interaction with her children. In the visions of Revelation, the martyrs are again clothed by God, in robes washed in the blood of the Lamb. It is all consuming, being a mother; it takes over the narrative about who we are and what we are about in the world. Although we certainly make our own impact on the world, now so do these others, nurtured in our image. All that waiting to become a mother was really waiting to give up control.

The creation stories in Genesis identify all of humankind as God's children, made in God's image. Yet a specific, intimate relationship that mirrors mother and child is quite different from God's general love for all people. For this, God waits. The pattern of God reaching out to chosen people in the ancestor stories of Genesis is like a series of adoption processes, only made official when the children live into the relationship, responding in trust. There is trauma too, as each of them loses connections with their birth families and former lives when they follow God into the future. Noah, Abraham and Sarah, Jacob, and eventually, Moses are each children whom God chooses, and who respond by allowing the relationship to define who they are. It takes a lot of waiting to get there. Were there false starts to God's parent-child relationships that we do *not* read about in the Old Testament? Did God just have to decide to move forward although the fit was questionable? Parents might love as unconditionally as possible. But the slow growth of mutual attachment strengthens us into the mothers we want to be.

Before reading Kelley Nikondeha's *Adopted: A Sacrament of Belonging in a Fractured World*, I had never considered how the relationship formed between Abraham and God resembles an adoption. Now I cannot see it any other way. The waiting is part of this story too, in multiple ways. God waits as Abraham uproots his family from the land of his ancestors and heads off at God's instruction. When God promises to make of him a great nation, he and his elderly wife Sarah scheme to conceive a child through Sarah's handmaid Hagar. Do not tell me this story makes the case that adoption does not last once a child-by-blood is in the picture, though. All it proves to me is that even the most revered patriarch and matriarch of our religious lineage messed up when it came to setting life-giving adoption boundaries and relationships.

The grievous power dynamics and lack of boundaries would make anyone involved with foster care or adoption shudder. Abraham and Sarah used their power over their servant Hagar to make her conceive a child with Abraham who would be "birthed on Sarah's knee," and therefore a legitimate heir. Genesis recounts that Sarah became deeply jealous of both the birth mother Hagar and child Ishmael once she had birthed Isaac, but I wonder if she had ever bonded with "her" child Ishmael, or always kept him at arm's length. Ishmael represented Sarah's own inability to conceive not just for her many years of marriage, but specifically as she saw her part in bringing God's promises to fruition. Sarah did not try to be the adoptive parent, as far as we can tell. Sarah is not the parent I have my eye on in this situation, anyway.

There is so much heartbreak in this story of who is to mother the promised child that we almost get distracted from the mothering activities God is doing: waiting while children attempt their own solutions, reminding them of promises and assuring them of God's ability to deliver on those promises. Our mothering God turns the heartache Abraham and Sarah have caused toward a new future. God claims and makes promises to the child Ishmael at Abraham's pleading. "As for Ishmael, I have heard you; I will bless him and make him fruitful and exceedingly numerous; he shall be the father of twelve princes, and I will make him a great nation. But my covenant I will establish with Isaac, whom Sarah shall bear to you at this season next year" (Gen. 17:20–21). Once Isaac is old enough to play with his half-brother Ishmael, the sight of them together stirs up the old resentment in Sarah. She wants Hagar and Ishmael gone, and God seems to realize that there is no repairing this complicated family dynamic.

> The matter was very distressing to Abraham on account of his son. But God said to Abraham, "Do not be distressed because of the boy and because of your slave woman; whatever Sarah says to you, do as she tells you, for it is through Isaac that offspring shall be named for you. As for the son of the slave woman, I will make a nation of him also, because he is your offspring."
>
> Genesis 21:11–13

Sarah would not do the work, so God would have to make a new way for Ishmael and Hagar. The followers of Islam, who share Abrahamic ancestry with Jews and Christians, testify to the great nation God promised to create from Ishmael.

This next part of the family story is of primary interest to only one of those three branches of faith rooted in Abraham: the Christians to whom I belong. God bringing Jesus into the world as God's own begotten child is the foundation of our faith. How long did God wait to become a parent by birth? Although many of God's interactions with Abraham and other chosen leaders resemble parenting, the analogy has some holes. For example, the leaders live into their relationship with God during their own adulthood. God experiences parenthood in a different way with Jesus's birth, a child who from the beginning knows he belongs to God. According to Matthew 1:7, "all the generations from Abraham to David are fourteen generations; and from David to the deportation to Babylon, fourteen generations; and from the deportation to Babylon to the Messiah, fourteen generations." What must that biding of time have been like for God, waiting to form the intimate relationship of parent to a helpless, vulnerable child? Was God waiting for the right timing, when the "family" was stable, or at a crisis point? Or for the right earthly partner in Mary? Did God wait for all the resources to be lined up, for this child to survive and become all he needed to be for the sake of everyone else? For what do we wait in planning for children?

Christians take a kind of comfort in reading the prophetic books of the Hebrew Scriptures as "foretelling Jesus" yet since the prophets declared their messages to their own time and place, we are always reading anachronistically. Still there is something about this tendency: what happened long before sets the stage for this and every birth. Even things we never noticed, like how we were parented or who was included in our family circle, subtly influence the families we envision or create. Maybe potential parents think we are waiting on the right time, the right conditions, to have enough money or a settled home or the right partner to have children. At least half of pregnancies are unplanned but are still a product of our histories and choices, or in some cases the choices imposed upon us by society. When a pregnancy is the result of rape, misogyny and toxic masculinity overshadow women's individual choices about having children. Living in such a society is still part of our story. Whether we planned it or not, this much is true: we did not get here alone, and we cannot move forward alone.

Jesus is a child of God in a different way than Adam and Eve, Abraham and Sarah, Moses or David. According to Christian theology, God depended on a human woman to bring the One fully of God's own being and yet fully human into our world. For this, God needed Mary's participation. How might we view this: God used a surrogate? Is God a previously arranged adoptive parent, foreshadowing with the announcement to Mary but making God's parentage official at Jesus's baptism in the Jordan River?

With Mary as Jesus's mother, then must we see God as Father (but—oops—Jesus has that in Joseph too)? Instead of attempting to definitively label the relationship, perhaps we can recognize that in waiting and depending on others to become a parent, God experiences as we do the necessity of letting go and trusting others, in order to take on this new role. Perhaps God had to acknowledge too: some of the characteristics the child gets from me will be problematic for them and some beautiful; the same will be true from my partner.

If we did not recognize the miraculous nature of women's bodies before, let this be the time. Women pastors and preachers are an embodied testimony to how much God trusts our bodies. God depends on a woman's body and waits on a woman's body to become a parent, the pinnacle of relationship with humankind. Not only do women's bodies expand and reshape to hold, nourish, protect, and bear humans into the world, but we believe that Mary's body bore the Divine. So much of our waiting on our bodies to conceive or carry to term can be fraught with worry or self-blame over genetics or behaviors. When an unplanned pregnancy brings risk and brutal hardships for the mother, we look for whom to blame. Does the claim that God entered our world and became an intimately invested parent through one such fragile yet powerful unplanned pregnancy change anything? That belief puts my own self-scrutiny to rest a bit because God trusted a woman's body to grow, deliver, and raise God's only begotten child, in a time when birth outcomes and survival to adulthood had frightening odds. God trusts and thanks Mary's bodily strength and resilience to birth and raise Jesus. How might our attitude toward women's bodies change, if we put this truth front and center? Women's bodies are miraculous, and are God's chosen means of entering our world!

Fertility Struggles

In the first creation story, Genesis 1:26–28 reads,

> Then God said, "Let us make humankind in our image, accord-
> ing to our likeness; and let them have dominion over the fish of
> the sea, and over the birds of the air, and over the cattle, and over
> all the wild animals of the earth, and over every creeping thing
> that creeps upon the earth." So God created humankind in his
> image, in the image of God he created them: male and female
> he created them. God blessed them, and God said to them, "Be
> fruitful and multiply, and fill the earth and subdue it; and have
> dominion over the fish of the sea and over the birds of the air
> and over every living thing that moves upon the earth."

Procreation is necessary to a creation story, to explain how there got
to be so many people from presumably two. God says, "Be fruitful
and multiply," and it sounds like a command for human beings to act
upon. Yet God does not say, ". . . if I decide to bless you with fertility." Our creation stories tell us who we are, establishing our identity in relation to the rest of creation and to God. There is nothing
in there implying "procreation is the major indication of the quality
of relationship between God and humankind" or "disregard caring
for creation as long as you make babies." In fact, "being fruitful"
and "multiplying" are two different verbs, so in addition to making
human beings, having lives that produce good fruit in the world carries just as much weight as the other verb. In any case, even if one
is determined to take this creation story as historical, there is still
no mention that God is going to be involved in conception or the
lack thereof. Eve offers an interpretation with the naming of her first
child, since the word for "produced" in Hebrew is similar to "Cain":
"I have produced a man with the help of the Lord" (Gen. 4:1b).

Language about God opening wombs or granting pregnancy
becomes a convention in scriptural stories (Rachel, Hannah, Mary),

making a case that God has a hand in the trajectory of our lives. Sarah laughed when she heard she would birth a child. It is not written that she begged or bargained with God for a child, but God promised and then gave. The idea of praying hard enough to over-come fertility struggles may come from what we remember of Hannah's story. In 1 Samuel, chapters 1 & 2, Hannah is one of Elkanah's two wives, and is constantly taunted by the other, rival wife. Hannah wept because of how she was taunted, and picked fights with her husband, who thought he alone should be more than enough to make her happy. Then she made a vow to the Lord that if she would conceive a child, she would give him to the Lord's service. Hannah made an adoption plan, even before Samuel was conceived. This is a key story to show how God cleanses the priesthood that had become corrupt. What if Hannah's story is not about fertility but about adoption? If anything, Hannah teaches us how children are not "ours" in the first place.

I am convinced that fertility is not actually the point in many of these stories, nor are they preaching some kind of fertility gospel of pleasing God to get pregnant. The detail that "God opened her womb" seems to be included in some stories so the next thing could happen, but not necessarily to say that previously God was actively closing a woman's womb. I have heard from individuals who are not able to conceive that perhaps God does not want them to be parents, and I fear that a misunderstanding of these plot points in the Bible might be at fault. Yet we do not blame other situations that cause us grief on God, do we? For example, does anyone claim that God does not want them to be employed, so is keeping them from finding employment? Does God keep some of our blood pressure too high, give some rheumatoid arthritis or others early onset Alzheimer's? Wouldn't we be ashamed to blame any of those things on God? So why, then, does infertility or conception get pinned on God?

One day when our older child was four, my body stretched and contracted, until, with blood vessels popping all over my face, I pushed our second child out into the world. The few times Scripture expresses a metaphor of birthing (most often in the prophetic book of Isaiah), the pain, effort, and power of a mother comes through. What I want to remember that God must know too, is that a mother should never have to muster that strength alone. She needs a partner, a midwife, her own mother, perhaps even a doctor trained in C-sections to help her find the strength to push her child out or to take over and get her child out. We need each other to birth new life. That, for me, was literally and metaphorically true. My maternity nurse Rose and my husband coached me through to the other side, past the utter absence of color that I saw behind my eyelids every time I clamped them shut to push, into living color once again. Knowing that my mother was at home caring for our older daughter, I entrusted myself to Rose's knowledge and experience and to my husband's firm grip. They stood by me and bolstered me through this most miraculous of actions. For women who must give birth via cesarean section, the help of others is the only way both mother and child survive.

Did the Holy Spirit get to midwife for Mary? Surely God did not instigate conception, then leave the birth to Mary alone. Several times in the Psalms God is described as acting like a midwife:

> Yet it was you who took me from the womb; you kept me safe on my mother's breast. On you I was cast from my birth, and since my mother bore me you have been my God.
>
> Psalm 22:9–10

> Upon you I have leaned from my birth; it was you who took me from my mother's womb. My praise is continually of you.
>
> Psalm 71:6

Would God not also be comforting and encouraging, pushing even (as the Holy Spirit often does), until mother and child are safely resting on the outside? Or perhaps the Holy Spirit is more like a postpartum doula, who helps the new mother to adjust after the birth, address the physical changes, mitigate anxiety about the new role, and navigate all the uncertainty? The Spirit of God might be manifested in the hormone oxytocin that flows through a new mother's body with great purpose. It gets labor going in the first place. Then a newborn scrambling to breastfeed releases more oxytocin, which increases a mother's feelings of attachment. God knows we cannot muster it on our own, especially after a traumatic birth. Breastfeeding or skin-to-skin contact get credit for stimulating the release of oxytocin, but we could also think of that hormone release as God no longer holding her breath. The wait is over, the pushing is finished, and the breath of life releases in a forceful wind. Now the mothering begins.

A birth mother's powerful actions during labor and delivery can set a precedent for understanding the mother's role in general. This is some of the groundwork the Old Testament prophet Isaiah lays in comparing God to a woman in labor. Lauren Winner has a remarkable chapter on this little-used metaphor for God in her book *Wearing God: Clothing, Laughter, Fire, and Other Overlooked Ways of Meeting God.* As mothers grunt, pant, or moan during labor in order to endure and manage it (although it cannot really be controlled), God too births the new creation through hard breathing and fierce labor.

We hardly ever talk about any of these things in church, but what if we did? The more vulnerable leaders are, the more our words matter. How many mothers' lives might we connect with? How many who are not mothers might value mothers' lives and witness in a new way? A male colleague told me how he nearly broke down while preaching on the divorce text from Matthew 19, as he talked about his own divorce and struggling with that scripture. People told him it was the best he had ever preached. Several women clergy I know have developed special worship services for those with fertility struggles, miscarriages and infant loss out of their own deep grief over such losses. If a clergy mother picks up her upset child during worship, every mother in the place knows what it is like to be so needed, and yet have to multitask for everyone's sake. What a gift that vulnerability is to others. So, I am working on seeing my overactive tear ducts as a blessing for ministry, to let myself share more vulnerably with others.

A dear friend of mine has written about her fertility struggles in *Still a Mother: Journeys through Perinatal Bereavement,* participated in podcasts, a documentary, and the creation of a stage play about the journey to become a mother. She has become a master gardener, tends her friendships well, is the best auntie to her nieces, and cares for a congregation as an Episcopal priest and marriage and family therapist. She puts her vulnerable self out there, so that others know they are not alone. She negotiates relationships from a position of authority and nurture all the time, mothering like God. This friend helps me to recognize those who mother without the formal or public acknowledgment of their actions. She debunks the word "infertile" for herself and many others who have not been able to birth children but are certainly leading fertile lives in a myriad of ways.

Being childless by choice can be a faithful way to live as well. Several friends who are teachers have chosen not to become parents because the nurturing of young lives they do for the better part of most of their days is clearly enough. A friend who is a woman of color has mentored into adulthood so many undergraduate students that they would need the auditorium at the predominantly white college where she was a vice president in order to fit all of her "children" into one room. A third friend welcomed into her home two young men whose parents passed away; their relationships were already established through the church's youth ministries, but she took their relationship much deeper. They call her Mom and visiting her is "coming home." Each of these loving people mothers with a constancy that reflects God's consistent care for us.

Before Jesus was born into the world, God's mothering identity was a metaphor we would not likely notice in scripture very often. We do not have to stretch it to make it fit every part of the Bible; all analogies break down at some point. "Lord" was the more common way of addressing with respect the all-powerful God in the Hebrew Scriptures. In those fourteen generations of waiting between Abraham and Jesus, God is not often described in ways that resemble a mother or father. In fact, at some points God tries methods of discipline that I shudder to think of a parent using with children they love. Sometimes we are not mothering either. We are doing good work that needs to be done for future generations even if they will not be "our" children.

If we check the verbs—of our actions and God's—we might just be parenting without the title. God heard their cries, instructed, lamented, grieved, cried out, warned, and disciplined her children in between redeeming them from slavery in Egypt and sending them into exile in Babylon. She yearned for them to listen and to turn back to her. These may not be the actions mothers are most proud of, but they can certainly be used to describe some of our activities. When the identity of parent is breaking down for God or for us, perhaps we are in a waiting period, when that deeply invested, caregiving identity is not primary but it is certainly not gone, just like for our friends who are not recognized as parents, yet are behaving in parental ways. To name that waiting and the variety of parental actions will allow many people to know that they are seen by their faith community and by God. For clergy women to give ourselves permission to speak honestly about the Wait can be a gift for open, mutual pastoral relationships.

QUESTIONS FOR REFLECTION

Clergy Women:

1. Which words or actions of others were most helpful to you, during periods of waiting for children?

2. How do you understand the Wait to become a mother to have affected your spiritual life or relationship with your congregation?

Support Network:

1. What has been your understanding of God's involvement in pregnancy or adoption? Have any of those ideas changed through reading this chapter?

2. Which of the ways God "became a parent" named in this chapter surprised you to think of it that way? Why?

3. Does it shift any of your expectations of God or your pastor, to acknowledge the pressures of the Wait?

CHAPTER 2

❧

Mama in the Center

In many families there is a parent who is treated like the president, and one who is the vice president. If the president is unavailable, the vice president will do. If the president is there, however, she (and it is most often "she") is the one the children go to for help, solace, or affirmation. The caregiver who bears that honor and responsibility may shift and change as our responsibilities outside the home change, but we all know who the president is in our family right now. This language and comparison came from a parent educator in the public school system, but the same could easily be said of our congregational life. Everybody knows who is at the center, and the Central One sets the tone for all the other relationships. Here's a clue: It is often the primary caregiver, the one doing the mothering.

Trust

None of us are born attached to our parents or caregivers. We are born needy, certainly. When a child's needs are met consistently by a primary caregiver, the child *seems* to establish a trust and bond with that caregiver (so often the mother). This bond is not innate; it comes through consistent care and affection, which is a great deal of work, especially in the middle of the night. It takes deep commitment to love and care for a child no matter what. Every. Single. Time. Parents must respond while carrying our own wounds, losses, upheaval, and even postpartum depression.

Postpartum depression can affect birth parents or adoptive parents, as it is intertwined not only with hormones and brain chemistry, but also with our own shifting identity. The reality of holding our children's lives in our hands is terrifying and more demanding than we could have imagined. Depression tells us we are not up to the task. Scripture portrays God having some of these responses too, regretting making humankind in the first place in Genesis 6:6–7: "And the Lord was sorry that he had made humankind on the earth, and it grieved him to his heart. So the Lord said, 'I will blot out from the earth the human beings I have created—people together with animals and creeping things and birds of the air, for I am sorry that I have made them.'" God's emotional responses to humanity can seem unpredictable too; sometimes anger surfaces quickly, or sadness. Postpartum depression is complicated and multilayered, but these details might connect God's experience to human responses of new parents. The Holy Spirit can speak through the honesty of others who have been through it, and even through the screening questions at our doctor's appointments. Thanks be to God that we are not alone.

While parents adjust to our new roles in an adoption, our children are navigating how to respond, too. Adoption psychologist Nancy Verrier describes a "primal wound" in the lives of adopted children whose first central relationship (with their birth mother) was broken. That severed attachment can become a defining characteristic, showing up later as a sense of loss, anxiety, or uncertain identity. Perhaps not all adoptees experience it: we all respond differently to our circumstances. Yet that this theory exists at all testifies that the relationship with our mother is central for most of us, to who we become and how we relate to others. Congregations might consider how their attachment to a founding pastor or one who shaped their most significant years echoes in this theory.

When my husband and I adopted our elder daughter, attachment was the primary initial focus of our lives. Prospective adoptive parents are counseled on how to establish that they alone are the ones their child should attach to in their new life, which can seem harsh to grandparents, friends and other caregivers. Parents must be the ones to meet all their child's needs for physical affection, emotional comfort, and basic needs like food. No one else, for six months, we were told. It was not a threat, to heed or feel guilty about (there are circumstances outside of our control). It was advice from those who know how delicate and difficult it can be for humans to form new secure attachments, to trust and live as though this new relationship will be forever. To do that, we need our focus narrowed down to only one or two people, until it sticks. There will be developmental stages, especially in the teenage years, when everyone questions their identity and belonging, but the goal we keep in front of us as adoptive parents is to pay attention to nurturing attachment and never to sow any seeds of doubt about the permanence of our family. As Paul writes, when we cry "Abba! Father!" it is the spirit bearing witness to our trust that God our Parent hears and will respond to us. Every single time. This is a permanent, secure attachment. Yet even with God, it takes time to develop attachment when we have been abandoned by others.

As I began my first solo pastorate, the contradictory advice from colleagues was rampant. Start out in the way you intend to continue. Carry on where the interim pastor left off. Remember: you only have six months to change everything that needs changing, while they forgive you because it is a "honeymoon period." Also, do not change anything for the first year, minimum. In reality, the initial challenge is to figure out with whom we are working and how we will build trust with them. One of my first actions as pastor was to attend a women's retreat, where I met all the "mothers of the church" at once. One of the West African women with a gregarious personality seemed to me like a main figure in the group, because she was so vocal. She volunteered information about many of her peers, and I began thinking: "She will be so helpful to me! I will consult with her and learn a great deal." I remembered her name and face, while others blended together in my memory. Yet I did not see her in church for nearly a month after that; she was not as much of an insider as I had guessed. I gradually learned that one of the least vocal women was the quietly dependable and revered leader among the African women of the congregation. I should not have assumed that figuring everyone out would be simple or possible. I also waffled quite a bit between trusting my instincts and doing what I was told was culturally expected by the West African church members. Stepping into this central role was such a privilege and a huge puzzle. How do we become the central figure everyone can depend on, knowing that someday the center has to hold without us?

Jesus most certainly struggled with this. His disciples were arguing about sitting at his right and left hand, when his face was set on Jerusalem, and he was trying to prepare them to go on without him. As any self-aware caregiver, Jesus knew that he was the center of the family they had formed, for each and every one of his disciples. Yet he would not always physically be there to hold them together. "Come and follow me. I will make you fish for people," he invited. Perhaps all some of them heard was "follow *me*." When we are new to the family, tuning into that primary relationship until it is firmly established is critical. Until we can trust the One, we are not much good at radiating the loving purpose of our family out to others. I bet Jesus's followers functioned as if Jesus was the "president." They may not have depended on him for everything, with meals and lodging likely arranged by the women, but for advice and reassurance and settling disputes and empowerment to do hard things and validation of being special and beloved, they likely turned to Jesus. He was the center of the family, like a mother.

A lot of a mother's time building trust is spent doing not much at all, or what seems like not much. We spend an inordinate amount of time meeting basic needs: feeding, dressing, and soothing. Yet while we are doing these things, are we silent? No, of course not. We are talking, making eye contact, noticing things about our children's bodies, asking about what is going on with them. We are practicing the care we hope our children will someday give others and teaching them how members of our family respond to hurt. Jesus's early followers—men and women—had lots of time with Jesus. The most notable incidents were remembered, retold, and eventually written down. Yet there were most certainly many mundane ordinary days that strengthened their bonds of trust. We like to focus on Jesus as otherworldly and therefore perfect, but he was also fully human, so his "children" in the faith probably also saw him cranky, tired of being needed by everyone, really looking for some help over here, and frustrated that they hadn't become independent yet.

There is so much touch involved in caregiving: carrying, holding hands, embracing, and rubbing someone's back as they calm down or fall asleep. It is astonishing how abruptly after reaching Mama's arms an infant can turn off the tears. Getting a couple to hold hands for mutual support during marriage therapy may change the dynamic significantly. Jesus uses the potent balm of touch among his closest "chosen family" and many others, all children of God. If Jesus feels the power go out of him as a hemorrhaging woman touches his garment, then he probably—like a mother accustomed to small hands reaching for her—recognizes that touch is a caregiving superpower. Jesus takes a young girl's hand, and thus raises her from the dead (Mark 5:41–42). He commands his disciples: "Let the little children come to me, for it is to such as these that the kingdom of heaven belongs," and by embracing them smashes cultural norms that devalue children until they are of an age to help support the family. Jesus hands Peter the fish he has cooked himself, on the beach after his resurrection. I imagine Jesus supporting the hand that takes it with a lingering touch, pressing the wounds from the nails into Peter's own flesh. When Thomas needs proof that the One in that locked room is indeed his beloved Jesus, he readily shows his scars, taking Thomas's own hand to place it in his side. Like a mama showing her C-section scar, the body cannot lie: I am yours. The power of touch works in both directions. To feel our hearts beating together while we hug can build attachment within the caregiver too and strengthen our mutual sense of loving and being loved.

Another way to interpret that incident with the bleeding woman—depending on Jesus's tone—might be exasperation: "Who is touching me now?" Clergy women talk among ourselves about being "touched out" from all the clinging of small children, hand-holding of elders, the handshaking/hugging line, and huddling up for youth group community-building exercises. When there are worshipers who give off sexually inappropriate vibes and insist on moving in for too-long hugs instead of taking the handshake offered, our bodies, *with which we do our ministry*, are at risk of feeling violated. Our bodies do not feel like our own, in real and vulnerable ways. This loss of personal space is magnified during pregnancy, when people might feel it is permissible to touch our expanding midsection. That identification with pastor as "part of our family" blurs their sense of decorum. Yet clergy mothers know that our availability builds the congregation's confidence in the Word we preach and the love we are attempting to fortify in our faith community and family. Sometimes it is too much. We want nothing more than to get on a boat and float away from the crowds for a little regrouping. (We know they'll be there whenever we get to the other side of the Sea of Galilee, but for just a little while, can we have a moment with fewer bodies reaching for us?)

Jesus's powerful touch and ours are not just about granting miracles. Sometimes it can seem that way. People ask me to pray for them, although I know their prayers are just as effective as mine. I want to believe that miraculous healing is not why people are drawn to Jesus, or why they return to church during crises. The power of being trustworthy is holding people, witnessing and participating in their pain during the non-miraculous times. Remember when

Jesus said, "The Son of Man has nowhere to lay his head"? He lived an itinerant, uncertain life in solidarity with our precarious lives. His physical body was touched to the point of death, until he was lifted up by God to new life.

Jesus's body was a significant part of his ministry of presence, building trust. But his words are most certainly trustworthy, too. They tell the truth about us, both painful and reassuring. When speaking with the Samaritan woman at the well (John 4), Jesus earns her trust by telling the truth about her marital history, which turns her into an evangelist for Jesus, the "living water." In the upper room during Holy Week, Jesus honestly identifies which of his disciples will betray him, then delivers to even Judas Iscariot his life-changing words that Jesus is giving up his own body and blood for us. His words do more than communicate; they establish a way people may come into direct contact with God on earth. His words are also actions, which can be trusted and should be repeated by us in remembrance of him.

From the start, caregivers telling the truth to us, about us, matters. Before we become teenagers trying to define ourselves against our parents, the trustworthiness of our central parenting figure sets the stage for how our relationship can recover from that inevitable defiance. For example, it matters that we talk to our kids about sex and how babies are made in age-appropriate ways from a young age, using the correct name for body parts. It is not the stork. If we are honest from the beginning, sharing bits of truth in matter-of-fact ways as they grow, what they are not able to process will go over their heads and what they need to hear, they will. What the children will most certainly understand is that they can talk to us about anything, especially the subjects that become fundamental parts of our identities.

For our children and within our congregations, two of the most crucial topics to be honest about are death and grief. Death is coming for us all, and even though we hope for the resurrection of the dead with Christ, grief is mighty powerful. We will all experience many kinds of loss, some of it accompanied by guilt, some by the pain of victimhood. More than anything, we need a God who will tell us the truth about that, weep for real, beg for that cup to be taken from him, and demonstrate that, even on the other side, wounds are still there. That is truth telling I can trust. Children of God do not need empty promises or the stifling attempts at comfort that prove the other person is uncomfortable such as, "Don't cry" or "God will make something good out of this." We need caregiving that tells the truth and is comforting because someone is in solidarity with us.

I was a teaching assistant for a freshman core class that encompassed Theology 101 among other subjects. I witnessed college freshmen who were so disturbed by reading the Bible and realizing for the first time that there are, in fact, two different creation accounts in Genesis that one young woman actually developed a kind of tic, a shiver. We talked about the different sources in putting the scriptures together. The assertion that those words were written in a way other than by holy dictation broke her. The faith community that raised her had reinforced repeatedly that the Bible was the unquestionable Word of God, so to read it as literature or more specifically as a compilation of multiple faithful sources raised serious questions about her home congregation's trustworthiness.

Even in congregations that teach an expansive view of the Bible, we may be withholding the truth about who our members are or what they are to be about, when we do not intentionally prepare people to be evangelists. Sharing the good news of Jesus Christ out loud is our mission, more so than perpetuating an institution or consuming religious services. If we do not equip and commission Christians with responsibilities to live the faith publicly and to share the gospel with others, we have not told the truth about who followers of Jesus are called to be.

We are most likely to become adults who can trust and be trustworthy, or to use the adoption term, to form secure attachments, if we have previously experienced them. This is why, when it is possible, foster care is replacing institutional care. For children who were cared for from infancy in a children's home or orphanage, those that are most resilient were somebody's favorite, despite the boundaries put in place to keep relationships "professional." We met one of our daughter's caregivers in the children's home from which we adopted her in Eastern Europe. The woman's eyes teared up as she helped us bundle up our daughter to leave, and it gave us hope that Viktoria would be able to securely attach, to trust us someday. She had been *specifically* loved. While institutional care might get the job done of physically caring for children and monitoring them for medical care, attachment can only be learned personally. It is not optimal for speech and development to have a large group of children supervised by rotating adults, but to learn this essential part of being human—relationships and trust—we certainly need a personal relationship.

This is why the single most effective way of bringing new members into a congregation is through friendship. We are members at our current congregation (although I periodically disappear to do interim work) because of one such friendship. When I left my last settled call without a new one, we visited this congregation not far from where we live, which we knew to be a bit more ethnically diverse than the average mainline Protestant congregation in Minnesota. I was two weeks from delivering our second child, and anxiously looking for a church where our 4-year-old could be happy. We showed up, and our daughter saw the smiling face of her friend from our Early Childhood Family Education class. Our daughter's mournful story, "Me cry [at] old church. Wanna be with Mama whole time," was quickly replaced with "Me like new church! Me run!" This was a much better story.

Relationships are key to belonging, but I will admit, as a mainline Protestant, I have ambiguous feelings about the Evangelical insistence on a "personal relationship" with Jesus Christ. Praise songs that seem to describe Jesus as my boyfriend make me uncomfortable, as does praying as if Jesus and I are buddies. We are not close in that way. But in the context of parenting, especially mothering, I think I am on board. In a personal relationship like parent and child, both people are changed. I trust Jesus Christ like I trust my mother, because she has grown and changed while parenting me, and loves me no matter what. We affect each other. Her personality has not gotten lost in our relationship, nor has mine, but we influence each other. I can trust her because the influence goes both ways. Isn't that the point of relationships?

Mothering is so often about setting the table, both literally and figuratively. In so many cultures, preparing food and cooking are women's household work. Perhaps we can remember the smell or taste of a mother or grandmother's specialties, twists on cultural favorites, or her own best recipes. Those olfactory memories smell like love. Perhaps what we are really remembering is belonging, being at the table where they watched out for us, provided for us, took care of our bodies while we felt it in our spirits. Perhaps this is what we are doing when churches give communion to anyone who reaches for it. We are setting a table for belonging, to know that the one feeding us belongs to us and cares for us, even if we cannot grasp the mystery of the Eucharist. We have mothering experience testifying to the belonging nurtured around a family table. That makes the relationship between Jesus's real presence and us gathered around the communion table abundantly clear. While teaching—catechesis—matters deeply, I would not want to sabotage the trust between us by making an age or instruction the requirement to eat.

Resiliency

Distrust lingers, with longer and stronger roots than we may ever know. Reading the accounts of adult adoptees warned us about behaviors our older daughter might develop as she figures out her identity during the teen years. My husband who is a family practice doctor repeats the adage, "When you hear hoof beats, think horses, not zebras." This is a reminder that causes are usually the ordinary things, not the exceptional ones, yet doesn't deny the exceptional part of her history and its potential repercussions. The same could be true of symptomatic behaviors in a congregation. If we are not conscious ourselves of the reasons why we respond to each other in a certain way, maybe it is time to work on some self-awareness exercises.

Parenting a child whose trust was broken by someone else or serving a congregation whose trust was broken by a pastor is a tricky business. There is actually a term for pastors who clean up after a predecessor has been removed for misconduct: an after-pastor. After-pastors and after-parents have to be resilient and self-aware enough to remember that "it is not about me." I can only be in charge of my own actions: communicate clearly and often, regulate and process my emotions offline, and be as consistent as possible. That is easier said than done. I have my own baggage that can sabotage me in that mission. However, the fluidity of a pastor's job can give us time and space for self-assessment and self-care.

How does God-at-the-center-of-the-family establish trustworthiness after our trust has been broken? Throughout the Old Testament, the story is that the covenant with God has been broken by the descendants of Abraham, who were blessed to be a blessing. Can children uphold a covenant relationship? Of course they will fail. Of course we do. So to them (us) it can feel like God has broken trust, even though it was humankind's fault. God's mercy is the route to healing for our conflicted parent-child relationship. As a Christian, I see the incarnation of Jesus as an act of extreme mercy, meant to reconcile us to each other and God our Parent. So how does God re-establish trust in ways we will be able to accept?

Each of the Gospel writers have a different emphasis, for different people to hear "Jesus is for you." For example, Luke emphasizes the frequency with which Jesus interacts with women and other people on the margins of the community. Those who are themselves marginalized and yearning for community will hear the gospel of God's love for us when Jesus rebukes the powerful and stands in solidarity with those who have been belittled, shamed, or excluded. My story of why I follow God revealed through Jesus will best rebuild trust in God among people whose baggage lines up with mine. God asserts unconditional love for us not only through the person of Jesus, but through our many testimonies to Jesus's life and resurrection, to repair the breach between God and us. God builds trust by helping us craft a story that people like us need to hear; thus we are uniquely qualified to bear witness to our own truth about God. God convinces the kids to rebuild trust in the family by using our own self-interest to care for each other. Well played, mothering God.

More so than other clergy, clergy mothers are apt to experience the stretch and pull of being the "Sandwich Generation." Our caregiving stretches to the generation after ourselves, and to our parents' generation as they age, both at home and at church. The administrative work, emotional decision making, and daily physical care still falls disproportionately on women, in both directions. When everyone is in need, the ones in the middle are stretched thin. This dynamic is painfully evident in some congregations too: tensions over space usage, worship styles, budget priorities, or the pastor's time between the elders and younger generations. It can take all our self-control to negotiate petty arguments with care, because we know that the real issue is a fear of being left behind. We may quote the prophet Joel at an opportune time, putting both generations demanding our attention in the same boat: "I will pour out my spirit on all flesh; your sons and your daughters shall prophesy, your old men shall dream dreams, and your young men shall see visions."

Independence

The end goal of parenting is to raise our children into independent adults, but sometimes we lose sight of the goal in the scramble to make it through the day. Similarly, in my ordination vows I pledged to equip the saints for ministry, to send them out being Jesus in the world. Yet in the midst of my attempts to minister to everyone's needs, perhaps I perpetuate their role as religious consumers instead of active disciples. Sometimes there is a watershed moment, an abrupt halt to our caregiving, that reminds us and them that we had intended to strive for independence. What happens when the center of the family has to drop out for a time? There is a revelation of how much is handled by our central caregiver. When a clergy mother is absent on medical leave, family leave, or sabbatical, a congregation discovers their own dependence, or has new opportunities for communal leadership. If a clergy mother should be put on bed rest, it is hard on everyone, especially with the risk and the sudden nature of it. In other scenarios, we can plan ahead, line up coverage, and train people to notice and take care of the details we usually track. Sudden medical leave provides a clearer view of our role, though. One clergy mother friend of mine admitted that it was almost more work to set up all the coverage for her to go on sabbatical, than it would have been to just stay and do it all herself. Like leaving a babysitter in charge, or a substitute teacher, we feel obligated to explain everything we normally do, all the idiosyncrasies and individual needs we navigate. That is the way of least disruption, but is disruption necessarily a bad thing? Perhaps we too need to let go of the illusion of control. Turning the world on its head is often how God works most clearly to change hearts and minds. The abrupt absence of the one who was holding it all together means that everyone else sees more clearly what needs to be done, and that they can do it. It is tempting to fill the gap with someone who can grab all the ends flailing in the wind and pull it back together. But where is the learning in that? When Mother is away, others step up, and hopefully not just for a season until they can drop it all on her again. Sabbaticals and maternity leave are an unbidden gift to a congregation's self-awareness. When Mother is absent, the Holy Spirit has room to blow through.

Following Jesus's crucifixion, his followers grieved and hid. The disciples talked among themselves and comforted each other. Jesus, who had cared for them very thoroughly, had told them they would have to go on without him, but they had not heard. They did not know they would be expected to act as his body in the world. They were stunned and unable to function, except for some of the women who knew the caregiving things to do for a corpse. When the women discovered that Jesus was alive—he had come back to them!—they had hope again, but their shared mission was forever changed. It could only move forward with the next generation of Christians commissioned at Pentecost. Jesus's bodily absence, then changed return, created a space for the Holy Spirit to work through his disciples for millennia. Think of the possibilities when our children and congregations receive the power of the Holy Spirit, because we have left room, to spread the good news on their own.

Mothers prepare our children to live beyond us. In 2 Timothy 1:5–7, the apostle Paul describes how faith can be passed down from our mothers and grandmothers: "I am reminded of your sincere faith, a faith that lived first in your grandmother Lois and your mother Eunice and now, I am sure, lives in you. For this reason I remind you to rekindle the gift of God that is within you through the laying on of my hands; for God did not give us a spirit of cowardice, but rather a spirit of power and of love and of self-discipline." By loving, holding, teaching, and coaching, the mothering actions of pastor-mothers prepare the generations to carry on the legacy of our faith. When they know how well they are loved for Christ's sake, those we have prepared will not be afraid. We have taught them to recognize the power of God within them, and the power to discipline their own actions.

QUESTIONS FOR REFLECTION

Clergy Women:

1. What do you struggle with or what gives you joy about being "in the center" of the family/congregation's life?

2. So much of how we lead/parent is embedded in how we were raised. How do you effectively learn to parent/lead those who were not raised as you were, and cultivate their trust?

3. What happened during a time that you stepped back from some parts of your mother or pastor role for a time?

Support Network:

1. What habits of a pastor do you perceive best cultivate your trust in the church? How might these relate to how you were raised or how you raise your own children?

2. Have you thought about pastoral care and mothering together? What expertise do you notice or imagine overlaps?

3. If you are in the "Sandwich Generation," what are your stories that relate to your pastor's competing priorities? If you are not, what role might you play in lifting some of the expectations and caregiving duties that do not need to be on the pastor?

CHAPTER 3

Unpacking "Like a Family"

"This church is like a family."

We say it like it is a good thing. This sentiment is repeated in rural, suburban, and urban settings, often in smaller congregations. Who could unpack it better than clergy women? The phrase is intended to imply warm feelings, a sense of belonging, and mutual support in a community that knows and cares for its members. This metaphor describes how members of the congregation helped us through struggles or accepted us when the rest of the world seemed hostile. We may also be saying that our sense of belonging in the congregation is comfortable, like old patterns and habits in an ever-changing world. Congregations can resemble families in other less positive ways too, however: hard to get into, unwilling to adapt to new ways of doing things, or mostly interested in taking care of ourselves. How can we explain the fullness of the metaphor in ways all our "family members" can hear?

Jesus fully embraced the metaphor of family for his followers, but not in the same ways we do. In his time and culture, the obligation of belonging within an extended family meant decisions were often made by default—family and family patterns of behavior eclipsed individual identity. To leave behind that family without burying your father was intensely shameful. To denounce mother and siblings in favor of disciples and other followers was an abrupt rebuke. To "hate" your family, in order to become part of Jesus's new family was to instigate traumatic loss for the sake of following Jesus.

When we preach or teach on those scriptures, it would be a shame to take the teeth out of them. One of Jesus's disciples said to him, "Lord, first let me go and bury my father," and Jesus replied, "Follow me and let the dead bury their own dead" (Matt. 8:21–22). "Let the dead bury the dead" is harsh, any way you spin it. To leave behind our family of origin is jarring, no matter what it was like to live with them before. This is true, in some respects, even when there was abuse or neglect. When we leave our family of origin, could the resulting destabilizing of our identities be a good thing? Might we act less entitled or more eager to make and keep connections because we have lost our initial support system? What does this have to do with following Jesus? This would be a great conversation to have with teenagers, who are coming into their young adult independence, and their parents. What do we hope for our family, for God's sake? Matthew 12:46–50 could be read as a slap in the face to Jesus's birth family.

> While he was still speaking to the crowds, his mother and his brothers were standing outside, wanting to speak to him. Someone told him, "Look, your mother and your brothers are standing outside, wanting to speak to you." But to the one who had told him this, Jesus replied, "Who is my mother, and who are my brothers?" And pointing to his disciples, he said, "Here are my mother and my brothers! For whoever does the will of my Father in heaven is my brother and sister and mother."

Clergy mothers are well positioned to preach on this passage, proclaiming that families hold together not by the fact of their common genetics, but through consistent, repeated actions. A family does not stay together by standing still, but by moving and changing as individuals change. The definition of who belongs in our church family also needs to be semi-porous, and determined by our values, not simply heritage. If you are seeking to do God's will, or are vulnerable and need our care, we should consider ourselves related. Additionally, like a foster family, in times when people are highly transitory, we can be prepared to act as temporary family to those who will eventually move on. A friend whose congregation is near a military base on O'ahu expects the make-up of the congregation to change every year. At their best, this congregation embraces new people quickly, acting as family for those who are far from their families of origin, then blesses people as they leave.

Another way I would preach on Matthew 12 is to talk about entitlement. Considering ourselves entitled to special access to Jesus (or having our agendas carry more weight) because of our history in a congregation or some other marker of our identity is not how the Jesus Movement is meant to work. Your family history or your position as a brother or mother used to matter a great deal. But Jesus says to every person on earth that God loves them unconditionally, so claims of special privilege become a hindrance instead of a help. See how Jesus rebukes the very mother who birthed him for trying to make a special claim on his attention? Wow.

Large crowds were traveling with him and Jesus turned and said to them, "Whoever comes to me and does not hate father and mother, wife and children, brothers and sisters, yes, and even life itself, cannot be my disciple" (Luke 14:24–26). Followers of Jesus have to be willing to put Jesus's mission above our own. This gives us much to examine about our decision-making processes in a congregation. Are we seeking to please the members, or position our money, time, and talents to serve God's most vulnerable? How do we prioritize?

There are dimensions of being "like a family" for our congregations that Jesus does not address but become familiar habits among people who have been around each other for a while. For example, we tend to associate homogeneity with belonging. Clergy have a unique position from which to address these habits, especially when we are new to a congregation and can innocently notice resemblances. For example, on what do you comment when you first meet a baby? Often the first comments are something about being adorable, then progress on to family resemblances: "He has your ears!" or "Who do you think she looks like?" It is easiest to focus on physical traits, before Baby has much personality to talk about, but is that the only reason our conversations veer in that direction? It gets awkward quickly when adoption is involved, and people remark: "I know this isn't possible, but she does seem to have your eyes."

Similarity might imply belonging, but it does not create it. Commitment creates belonging, in a family or a church family. We choose, over and over again, to belong to one another regardless of what comes up. Do you ever get the sense that those who are "born into" our church family—and therefore may look or act like previous generations of its membership—are perceived to fit better than anyone who does not (new immigrants, same-sex couples, transgender persons, adoptive families, and so on)? Visual homogeneity can lull us into a false sense of comfort. We may even tiptoe around sensitive issues in order to maintain the appearance of unity. Once our real differences are uncovered, however, it can feel like a betrayal since we assumed we were "the same." At least when we do not look alike, we may more easily admit that to belong to one another is going to require work. Family resemblances do not make church families function, any more than they strengthen household families. Opting in and putting effort into creating those bonds makes a family.

In mainline Protestant congregations, we love infant baptisms. It is our theology that God does the saving and claiming of us, so children do not need to be able to choose the relationship to be marked as beloved children of God. Those baptisms may present opportunities to speak about our comfort with new members coming to us as children, because they fit so seamlessly into who we already know ourselves to be as a "church family." We get to imprint upon them our ideas of the right way to worship, participate in education, volunteer, or take part in the umpteenth annual ethnic heritage supper, and they believe this is how church is and ever shall be. They do not enter the family agitating to change it or challenging our ideas of who we are and what is most important to us as adult converts might do. But that is not exactly true, is it?

In our adoption process, my spouse and I knew that older children are harder to place, so decided we would be open to children up to age six, setting that limit largely for ease of language acquisition (since we were adopting internationally) and for our child to start school at the same age as their peers. Those were our parameters to make it easier on our child, but also, if we are honest, to make the transition easier on ourselves. We thought that children younger than school age have a better chance of blending in, catching up, and assimilating. As one parent said in a support group we were a part of, "We knew we were signing up to be a conspicuous adoptive family, but we didn't know we were also becoming a 'special needs' family." Some of those invisible needs that are never going to show up in the paperwork manifest later as behavioral, emotional, or cognitive challenges. Older children come with more history, and if they are in the care of the state, that likely entails neglect or abuse. The older they are, the more aware children might be of the emotional trauma of the whole story that led to them being available for adoption.

So it may be for some of those who come to faith or to our specific congregation from a different denominational background or church culture. They might be joining our church family because they have suffered neglect or some form of abuse in another church or tradition. If this is the case, I hope we are attentive enough to recognize that this is not going to be easy on any of us, and the whole family might change as a result. I hope we create the space for our newer family members to process what they have been through, as needed. We must create a safe space for them to tell us how our patterns exclude them. New members could be mirrors leading to self-awareness and renewal for our church family. Assimilation needs to be set aside as a goal, as we put all our effort instead into cultivating belonging for everyone. Resembling each other, except in sharing the love of Christ, is not a defining feature of the family Jesus created. Neither is fitting in without friction or requiring no adaptation by anyone else. When we read the New Testament letters about conflicts between Jews and Gentiles in the early church, it would be a natural time to discuss this hard work of bonding. The integration of Jews and Gentiles into one early "church family" was not easy or natural. Both Jewish and Gentile followers of Jesus needed constant reminders that what they had in common could and should overpower what was different. The obvious similarities were not there. Since they neither shared the lineage of the Jewish tradition nor resembled each other in many physical ways (including circumcision) they had to name those differences in order to get to the core that could hold them together.

Many of us have never considered that to embrace others as family will involve hearing about how we or others like us in the church have ignored or excluded them in the past. Yet we may hear this from families formed after trauma and loss, people struggling with mental and physical disabilities, financial hardship, or discrimination based on race, gender, or sexuality. This is why confession and forgiveness are a core part of our life together. The struggles of our siblings in Christ are our struggles and the understanding of God and God's people that emerge from these lived experiences can open up our "family's" theology in surprising ways. In our globally connected world, the notion that "we don't need to address that because we don't have any of *those* people here" has never been less true, regardless of the specific issue. Our claim to be part of the family of God falls flat if we operate on theology that only acknowledges or offers grace for some of us.

There is an incredibly tender moment of care at the end of Jesus's life, which I sometimes frame as Jesus making an adoption plan for his mother and closest friend. When Jesus saw his mother with the disciple whom he loved standing beside her, he said to his mother, "Woman, here is your son." Then he said to the disciple, "Here is your mother." And from that hour the disciple took her into his own home (John 19:25–27). Jesus is doing the most heart-wrenching mothering action I can fathom, handing off the care of his beloved family members, because he knows he will no longer be capable of caring for them. As we age, our caregiving is meant to reverse, and we children take care of our parents as they become the vulnerable ones. Jesus could not do that, so he told his mother and beloved disciple how he envisioned them living without him, by having each other. Might we also consider in this moment his sacrifice as a caregiver whose mothering actions have defined his life? He will no longer be able to teach and heal and advise and hold close all his beloveds. The loss is almost greater than losing his life. "After this," the very next verse says, "Jesus knew that all was now finished."

Mary and John must have felt the gravity of the sacrifice, for Jesus to give up mothering. Yet they still had their own interpersonal dynamics. Perhaps they got on each other's nerves or felt competitive for Jesus's attention. Maybe they wanted to be close to Jesus, but perhaps not particularly each other. Do you ever feel like that (church would be great if it were not for the people)? Maybe we committed to a faith community in order to be close to Jesus but end up caring for each other. Or the opposite happens—we join because a community surrounded us when we needed it, then we meet Jesus through them.

Paul used the language of adoption to describe how becoming God's children changes our lives:

> For you did not receive a spirit of slavery to fall back into fear, but you have received a spirit of adoption. When we cry, "Abba! Father!" it is that very Spirit bearing witness with our spirit that we are children of God.
>
> Romans 8:15

However, fear and trauma do not just go away for any of us. The PowerPoint slide that hit me the hardest at a recent fundraiser for an adoption medical clinic was the one that simply showed a family holding hands and a caption that read, "A family is the best place to heal." When that basic fear of not belonging to anyone is addressed, we open the doors to so many other kinds of healing, spiritually but also socially and even physically. I do not ever want to interpret Romans 8 as saying that trusting in the "spirit of adoption" means we no longer fear. I do not think it is meant to shame those who are afraid. Fear is what makes us cry out to God as our responsive parent: "Abba! Father!" Children of God still have many reasons to fear, and layers of trauma from what we have endured or will experience even while living into God's family. Yet we have someone to cry to, and that makes all the difference.

Paul continues: "and if children, then heirs, heirs of God and joint heirs with Christ—if, in fact, we suffer with him so that we may also be glorified with him" (v. 17).

Another adoptive family we know is very honest about the heartbreaking circumstances that led to the formation of their family. Their children's birth parents both died of diseases that were preventable, if they had had access to medical care. Their children now have a future where perhaps that particular risk is not such a threat. Yet all adoptive parents should bristle at the notion that somehow we "saved" our children, which is language better used to describe Jesus's actions rather than our families. Adoption only comes out of brokenness, that much is true. In this country or abroad, brokenness abounds. We did seek to do some good in the world by adopting a child who needed a family. Being in a family is a mutual relationship, however, and we are all changed by our life together. A savior complex puts a barrier between parent and child that denigrates our child's identity and questions the love that transforms us both. We committed from the beginning to suffer together and to be glorified together.

Churches may function in a similar way, because some people find a church home or return to church when they desperately need a support system. This is less often the case than it used to be, since church no longer plays such a prominent cultural role as a public institution. Yet some people still turn to us when they have nowhere else to go. It changes the church to have to grapple with what their presence and their need means to us. Are they "using" us? Do we make them play by the rules or assimilate to get help? How can our support be relational as well as financial, and what happens when someone's relational needs are more than we can handle? The "spirit of adoption" pulls and tugs at the hearts of church insiders, who get our faith and self-understanding stretched in new ways by the new children of God in our midst and what our interactions say about us.

Finally, Paul pinpoints a truth we do not often acknowledge: the ways human beings embrace or do not embrace each other as family has dramatic consequences for all of creation.

> For the creation waits with eager longing for the revealing of the children of God; for the creation was subjected to futility, not of its own will but by the will of the one who subjected it, in hope that the creation itself will be set free from its bondage to decay and will obtain the freedom of the glory of the children of God. We know that the whole creation has been groaning in labor pains until now; and not only the creation, but we ourselves, who have the first fruits of the Spirit, groan inwardly while we wait for adoption, the redemption of our bodies.
>
> Romans 8:19–23

The world's most vulnerable—whom Jesus refers to as his "little ones"—are the first and worst sufferers from natural disasters, which have intensified with climate change. Drought, destructive flooding, rising sea levels, the control of natural resources, and the rise of extremist movements fed by despair are major factors in displacing people worldwide, scattering them as immigrants and refugees without the safety net of home and family. Nobel Peace Prize winner Malala Yousafzai collected essays from multiple young women about their lives as displaced people, naming the book *We Are Displaced*. The key to Jesus's family being moved by these stories is not just in evoking empathy and compassion for others, guiltily feeling "there but for the grace of God go I." It is happening to *us*. Creation is groaning for us to act. Millions of displaced people are also part of us; we as God's children belong to each other, so we cannot tolerate our government refusing to address the root human (and corporate) contributions to climate change. How could I not speak out, push and advocate for change until my family are protected from further ravages and helped to recover?

There is bound to be groaning. This scripture passage summons collective groans from both labor pains and the pain of waiting for adoption. All children cause parents to groan, both in the waiting to become a family and within our relationships throughout our entire lives. What I would love to hear within a "church family" is the collective groan of those who know we are not complete in our homogeneity, without groan-inducing transformation from relating to those who challenge us. The Spirit cries out for adoption to bring us together with others as with God our Parent. We have not yet embraced all our siblings, stood with them against the forces of destruction, nor loved them so fiercely no one would dare challenge the lasting bond between us. We have not yet been transformed into the family of God that bonds together to care for the entire creation until we seek out those relationships that will challenge everything we assumed about ourselves.

How a Church Is Not Like a Family

Every metaphor, every analogy, breaks down at some point. Just as God the Father or Mother is a metaphor that does not always describe God, "family" does not always fit, or in fact sometimes obscures what the church is about. To begin, the relationships within a healthy congregation have to be more fluid than in a family. It should not be so difficult to get into and establish belonging. A dear elderly member of one congregation I served chuckled and told me (several times) that he "only married into" that congregation, sixty-five years prior when he married his wife. Imagine still defining yourself as an outsider after all that time. Perhaps we ought to ask ourselves if the confirmation photos on the wall or the ways we talk about our traditions are perpetuating the impression that one has to be born into this congregation to ever fully belong. Congregations can also benefit greatly from healthy goodbyes, beyond those we say at funerals. As members or even pastors move on, we may graciously release them with Godspeed to other parts of the church throughout the world, emphasizing how healthy it is for our membership to be porous.

Our mission as a faith community is to worship God and love our neighbor, so getting embroiled in family drama (over how we should do things) distracts from our purpose and keeps others on the outside. I suppose there are people who see a contentious system and either think they can help or see an opportunity to assert their power. The only way for a congregation to remain detached from our own agendas and arguments is to keep bringing our gaze back to the cross. We struggle to keep Christ at the center of our life together, although that is the only way to actually be his body in the world. Our reason for existing as a church is not for the sense of belonging created for our members, whether in trying to make everybody "inside" happy, or in strategies to perpetuate what we have going here. Faith communities exist primarily to prepare our members to live their faith out in the world, not to serve the family within. Certainly, inside the church should be a safe place to practice our acts of service, speak about our faith, and question alongside others. Still, the system does not exist to nurture itself, as much as it does to send us out to love the world. Maybe this is not a full departure from the "church is like a family" metaphor after all, as going out into the world is hopefully what parents raise our children to do.

Congregations must actively fight homogeneity and prejudices. While families reward assimilation and individuals develop their own roles to survive in a family system, Christians will only become Jesus's body in the world by diversifying our experiences and being changed by folks outside of our circles. Those outside of "the family" are key to the church becoming whom God would have us be. We will need to educate ourselves, and actively reject the "family-like" function of congregations perpetuating discrimination and prejudice. Jemar Tisby's 2019 book *The Color of Compromise: The Truth about the American Church's Complicity in Racism* identifies how white congregations perpetuate racist ideas and practices historically and contemporaneously. Erin Wathen's 2018 book *Resist and Persist: Faith and the Fight for Equality* uncovers the roots and systems that oppress women still within Christianity. These books felt for me like reading the hidden parts of a family history, and cringing at the resonances.

Instead of a family system, sometimes it helps to think about a congregation as a living organism, with a life cycle. When her life has been lived, we may need to let her go. I once helped to close a congregation and tried to frame the closing not as a failure but as faithfulness. We made the best decisions we could at the time so that her legacy would live on, celebrated her milestones, gathered everyone around to remember, and tried to provide some closure. We need to be good stewards of the resources a congregation consumes, such as money and people's energy and attention. We sent those resources out to have a life beyond her, once the congregation closed. But I wonder if that inner circle of people who were left at the end hung on too long because their sense of loss was so akin to losing family: a family who had bonded together through great challenges. I wonder if, by that point, they were so burnt out that many of them were taking a break before finding a new church home. Some of those breaks are likely to become permanent, as the research describes a growing demographic of formerly active church lay leaders now categorized as the "Dones." Church is not a family, because we do not become orphaned if our specific congregation closes, or we are estranged from it. There are so many additional ways to connect with the body of Christ in the world that the most meaningful congregation in your life perhaps prevented you from exploring. By all means grieve, but not as people who have no hope or family.

Church does not have to look like what we once knew for it to be the body of Christ on earth. In fact, as we reinvent church for generations burned by or who have simply had little contact with organized congregations, it makes sense to start with people's spiritual hunger rather than traditional models. It is a movement, not a household family; if we want to be part of it, we have to recreate church on our feet.

When the Pastor Cannot Be Like a Mother

I have not been part of any congregation since its beginning. Even in the case of founding pastors, they likely have not single-handedly nurtured the faith of every church member since their infancy. We each will someday need to leave the congregation in the capable hands of the next pastor. We tend the faith of those who have already been shaped by others' leadership and will be shaped by others after us. Since I have been working as an interim pastor, I have come to understand well that the pastor who served most recently may not even be the most influential in current dynamics, but those who stay too long certainly establish a culture. Because I know that I am one in a succession of pastors, I also do not carry full responsibility for the future of the congregation. The lay leaders must cast the vision, so I can help them head toward it. Pastors establish boundaries in the transition to a new phase, both for themselves and for the congregation they serve.

My ordination is not to mothering a congregation, but to preach, teach, preside over the sacraments, and equip the saints for ministry. My accountability is not to the health or well-being of the individuals per se, but to the Word of God we hear through scripture and experience through the power of the Holy Spirit working among us. More often than not, those are unsettling influences, if we resist watering them down and domesticating them. It is not about "meeting the needs," actual or perceived, of all congregants. We cannot, like a family, take funds from the budget to help every member in crisis. Neither should our budgets be exclusively about what those of us here want. The Word of God calls us to live for others, to tend the most vulnerable and seek justice for the oppressed, who may be primarily outside of our membership. That is not always popular. Congregations can react jealously to the perception that the pastor is putting others' needs for her time or compassion before their own.

While I could name ways each of the charges of ordination align with mothering, there is no escaping that pastoral ministry is also a job. The congregation (or campus ministry, chaplaincy, and so forth) pays me, and that affects our relationship as well. Exchanging pay for services can create a desire for measurements and lists of the details of relationship-tending. When a congregation does that, demanding a weekly recounting of people contacted or visited by their pastor, accounting for time spent in reading, ruminating, connecting those with similar interests or praying, we all know things are going downhill, and trust has been lost. The family metaphor may help us reclaim an understanding of the relational nature of ministry and to sort through our roles together.

QUESTIONS FOR REFLECTION

Clergy Mothers:

1. Which of Jesus's efforts to redefine family do you respond to most strongly? Why?

2. When have you experienced the "church is like a family" analogy as helpful or harmful?

3. How do you, as a pastor-who-mothers, approach integrating new members into a congregation?

Support System:

1. Which of Jesus's efforts to redefine family do you respond to most strongly? Why?

2. What cultural/family resemblances do you talk about in your family or church? How might emphasizing these traits build or detract from different individuals' sense of belonging?

3. Consider your experiences of leaving or joining new congregations. When did you know you belonged (if you did)?

CHAPTER 4

❧

Scrutiny (and the Ministry of Unseen Details)

I recently made my four-year-old skip her nap so we could attend the memorial service for a friend's mother. During the service, my little one was a bit whiny, stage-whispering three separate times, "This is boring. When is it going to be over?" I held her in my lap, kept the lollipops coming one after the other, and responded each time, "Just a little bit longer, then you can have one of those cookies over there." Afterward, our friend's spouse commented how she was "good as gold" during the service. "She goes to a lot of church," I replied, but I should have said, "I made it so." She had me all to herself, I was plying her with treats and talking soothingly, letting her use me like furniture. What may have seemed like compliance from her definitely took effort from me.

This is the same child who completely melted down in the central aisle during a special holiday service, instead of joining the few other kids present for a children's message with our (first female) bishop. My child acted as if she has no experience with church services or women pastors and, in fact, found them threatening and painful. I had coached her shortly before about what was expected and promised cookies after church. Her older sister ambled happily up to the front of the sanctuary. Immediately after I led our youngest child out of the pew, she threw herself on the ground, screaming, "No, I won't go up there!" After I had dragged her flailing body back to our pew and soothed until the end of the service, well-meaning people promised me, "someday you'll laugh about this." Believe me, I'm trying. Heh. Not yet? Maybe later.

All this is to say, what others observe about how my family behaves may have considerable stage direction behind the scenes by yours truly. Yet they may still act as though they are not at all familiar with church or the love of Jesus. As a pastor, I also have hopes for how congregation members will interact with each other or neighbors in our community, but even less influence over how they carry our reputation out into the world than I have within my family. I don't anticipate grown adults throwing tantrums in public, but judgmental stares or exclusionary political stances can make just as memorable an impression as my daughter's spectacle. Sermons, Bible study, and taking regular opportunities to define terms are all part of a pastor's preparatory work for the public witness of our congregation members. In the end, being the church is the mutual work of the people, and we influence each other's beliefs and actions. That does not necessarily reduce a leader's attempts to mitigate problematic theology or insensitive actions, but offers some grace when leaders take too much credit or blame upon themselves.

Clergy women are hyperaware about representing an entire demographic for people who have never seen a woman preacher or pastor before, much less a mothering one. I recall being warned by a woman seminary professor, "You know, you'll have to be twice as good as a man," and thinking, "That's fine, I can do that." But can we acknowledge and cite that unfair standard? The journalists doggedly asking male candidates for public office, "Who is taking care of your kids?" are laughed at, but their point is made: the moms get asked that all the time, so why shouldn't the dads? Clergy moms are overfunctioning on several fronts, when responsibilities for the congregation or childcare are not shared, because we know how much behind-the-scenes work is necessary to present a decent public face. Perhaps we need to learn to let go, to trust that our reputations and authority will remain strong even if we do not personally manage to keep everything running smoothly at home or at church, but experience has not proven that to be true yet, so we are wary. A pastor's respectable public image is part of leading, and being considered trustworthy, yet so is vulnerability. The trouble is I am not the only one representing me to the world. So are my children, and even my spouse somewhat (people attribute his late or rumpled appearance to my neglect, whether they should or not). I do not appreciate fielding criticism of my family or congregation, but if constructive criticism helps us to better love our neighbors, I am here for it. If it simply means that we do not behave according to expectations, I will let it go.

Matters that may seem small to parishioners can drive others away from a congregation: how someone's gender or relationship status is assumed, the suggestion that children are not well behaved enough in worship, or racist or sexist micro-aggressions that subtly find their way into small talk during coffee hour. I can proofread the bulletin and newsletter to make sure there are no egregious typos and no announcements are forgotten. I can keep up the family's blog or the church's website. I can clean out the fridge at home or at church when it is too disgusting to leave it that way. No one is likely to credit me for the time or effort it takes to do these things, and I wonder what it has to do with my role, anyway? Am I just the only person who notices? It is easier for me to take care of it than repeatedly ask others to do it. I really need to spend my behind-the-scenes effort and understanding on prepping the relational interactions. I need to be reading articles, books, and blogs by people who have been marginalized by their experiences with church people. I may not be able to get the church book club to read books on controversial topics, but I certainly need to read them to inform my own coaching, leading, and preaching. Romans 14:13–14 has a helpful ring to it:

> Let us therefore no longer pass judgment on one another, but resolve instead never to put a stumbling block or hindrance in

the way of another. I know and am persuaded in the Lord Jesus that nothing is unclean in itself; but it is unclean for anyone who thinks it unclean.

Managing the staff of a congregation can demand time and skill. The relationships between office manager and musician, interns and youth directors, plus their interactions with congregation members develop independently until there is a crisis. That is when pastors or priests may be called in. In parenting, I am sometimes at a loss to determine whether I should turn a conflict back to my children to negotiate on their own or intervene. The same tension exists among adults, when the overall health of the congregation is my business. I have messed this up more than I want to admit. I feel like all mothers might need to talk about our role in conflict management. We cannot force everything to be perfect so that others' impressions of us or our family are universally positive. But where do we draw the line on what to address? Conflict is part of relationships, but how we address it is the skill we are all learning as we go.

Pastors are called to be connectors—and the mental space and time spent connecting our congregation members to resources, or those with similar interests to each other, is significant. Loneliness is the scourge of our time, yet congregations have the potential to forge meaningful relationships among those in similar demographic categories and across generations or other divides. How often do we resist authentic relationships and vulnerability out of a habit of only showing our "Sunday best" to each other, until our needs are extreme? The work that I am most proud of lately is lifting up other writers and connecting them to opportunities to publish and present their work. There is no commission for that, but perhaps it falls under the role of pastor. Whether we connect those in our care to others organizing around their passions, or connect those in need to resources, the introductions are what make new relationships possible.

The Case Study

There is power in acknowledging that the clergy mother's family is being monitored. We can use that attention to teach about sexism, about the normal struggles of families today, about how to welcome and support children with specific needs. Since clergy mothers know—and can count on—that heightened visibility, we can build up our support systems to lead the work. We must find ways of processing our thoughts and feelings with trusted listeners outside of the congregation. Within our congregations, we have a unique opportunity to introduce crucial conversations.

Multiple congregations have become explicitly "open and affirming" toward LGBTQ folks because the pastor's child came out. While these changes are not without emotional effort, the opportunity is certainly there, especially when the clergy family is the case study. Clergy mothers present the opportunity for congregations to examine how we treat working moms, children, and teens. Others of us may have added "bonus" icebreakers because of other aspects of our identities such as body image, sexual orientation, gender, race, or background. While it may be painful for all involved, it can be a wonderful thing when a congregation learns and grows because the pastor's family opened their eyes to the necessity of welcoming people who are marginalized.

There are multiple sides to every interaction. What effect do we want our actions to have on people? Are we conscious of the potential to offend, or are we working intentionally to understand and potentially be changed ourselves? To begin rather benignly, I am teaching my young children to listen rather than talk when others are speaking. I am also teaching them that their voice matters, and church is a place they are welcome and appreciated. What is the higher value, and how can we all work together in a congregation to teach children both "how to do church" and that they are part of shaping our faith community? How does this same conversation extend to our welcome of folks on the autism spectrum, with developmental disabilities, or who have simply never been in church before? We may indeed have different interpretations of what is appropriate in a sanctuary, a faith community, or an individual's faith journey, yet our value is to listen to each other so we can decide how we want to communicate to families about their welcome among us.

God's guidance of humankind follows a similar trajectory. Let us return to the story of Abraham as the original chosen child of God. God makes promises to Abraham and directs him to leave his people in order to go forth into a future God will unfold through him. Yet not trusting God to take care of his relationships with the power brokers in that land, Abraham lied to those whose land he traveled through and his own family not once, but twice (Gen. 12 and 20) about his wife Sarah being his sister. Now, Abraham's a grown adult; isn't it a bit patronizing to compare his behavior to a child in need of a parent's correction? That is often how it feels when one in authority calls us out for our bad decisions made out of fear. We do not like the correction, but we need it. God has built up trust, and repeated this narrative with Abraham many times: You are my chosen child, I will be with you to protect you, I will give you the land I intend for you, and prosper you. (That means you do not need to scheme and lie about your wife being your sister, so that I have to afflict the pharaoh of Egypt or King Abimelech of Gedar with plagues for them to leave her alone.) God and Abraham have to have this talk twice. We may need correction for our actions as adults too.

Somebody is always watching. Observing the way "children of God" behave forms people's impressions of us, and by association, of God. God understandably rebukes Abraham, "You have done things to me that ought not to be done" (Gen. 20:9). Like Pharaoh and Abimelech, the audience for our errant behaviors will want answers, want to see us put in our place, and to have restitution if they have been wronged. Restoring healthy relationships will likely be draining, costly, and awkward; see the rest of Genesis 20. Yet here is the hope: after we get through responding to the behavior and trying to understand the fears behind how we have acted, maybe we all are in a deeper kind of relationship. What if we invited constructive criticism as a way of being faithful?

Clergy in my denomination and others are required to complete at least one unit of CPE (clinical pastoral education) before ordination. The visible work of CPE is providing spiritual support as a chaplain to people under stress in an institutional setting such as a hospital, nursing home, or prison. The work within ourselves during that time is perhaps more formative. We meet with a group of peers and present verbatim accounts of an encounter we had with someone for whom we attempted to provide pastoral care. Our peers and a supervisor ask us questions about why we think we reacted in a certain way. It is coaching to become self-aware. If participants have not been in therapy before, this required self-reflection and self-awareness can be painful, shockingly vulnerable, or at least uncomfortable. My congregation has not experienced CPE. They have not practiced questioning why they reacted to a person or circumstance in a certain way, for good or ill. We can model these things. The perceived "softness" of talking about our emotions is still more expected from women than men, so people may be more open to it from women clergy. There is inherent risk, of course, in showing vulnerability or admitting experiences in our past that may affect our current actions. To some, vulnerability makes one unfit to lead, but Jesus's words and actions testify that vulnerability is part of our theology. When we model thinking through our actions, addressing our prejudices or influences, we are coaching our people on how to move forward with intentional choices.

The eighteenth chapter of Matthew is full of strong direction for how to respond to the things the clergy mother's family or congregation is doing that bother somebody.

At that time the disciples came to Jesus and asked, "Who is the greatest in the kingdom of heaven?" He called a child, whom he put among them, and said, "Truly I tell you, unless you change and become like children, you will never enter the kingdom of heaven. Whoever becomes humble like this child is the greatest in the kingdom of heaven. Whoever welcomes one such child in my name welcomes me. If any of you put a stumbling block before one of these little ones who believe in me, it would be better for you if a great millstone were fastened around your neck and you were drowned in the depth of the sea. Woe to the world because of stumbling blocks! Occasions for stumbling are bound to come, but woe to the one by whom the stumbling block comes!"

Matthew 18:1–5

What if we are all those treasured children Jesus defends with such severe language? What if the warning about creating stumbling blocks for us children is paramount, and direct conversation—instead of triangulation—is really the way to begin? I am not ashamed to be thought of as a child compared to Jesus. It is a beloved, protected status. Here is where clergy mothers can lead with humility. We apologize when needed and ask for restitution when warranted, but always point to the truth that we are each beloved children of God.

As a clergy mother, I do not share criticism from the congregation with my spouse or children. There is already a tension created by the time I spend with the faith community, away from them. I will not put myself on the side of a congregant criticizing them. I must be for my family, first and foremost. If critics refuse to engage in a deeper conversation of values around caring for people with behaviors they do not approve of, the most they can hope for is that they will add another burden for me to wrestle with on my own.

The Risks

Wouldn't it be wonderful if a team of people—including clergy mothers—brainstormed ways to actively support parents and families in our faith community? None of us should carry full responsibility for the family or the community of faith on our own. We bear one another's burdens; we hold each other up and work for the common good. No individual—including clergy and other leaders—should be held responsible for all the behind-the-scenes details, up-front public presentations, and the behavior of anyone beyond themself. The pastor is not the church; the mother is not the family. We are all in this together. If we will not recognize the pressure we put on clergy mothers and others, their multilayered roles are unsustainable.

In a 2013 Barna survey of pastors' kids, the results were overwhelmingly average. By the percentages, PKs are just as likely to rebel or be model churchgoers as their peers. The survey also seems to present normative self-reporting about clergy parenting, compared to those in other career fields: attributing some of their children leaving the church to their own busyness or lack of modeling faith at home. While that may be shocking coming from a person responsible for the faith development of an entire congregation, it is certainly a parallel to the time spent away from our families by parents in many career fields. There is also a recurring theme of "I didn't sign up for this" from pastors' kids. They had no choice about being in the spotlight. It certainly could not hurt to acknowledge that, so that congregation members—as well as our children themselves—recognize the stereotype and potential bias.

The joke that causes pastors to cringe but congregants tend to think is hilarious goes like this: "You only work on Sundays, right?" *Sure*, just as God is only working when we see the words "Lord" or "Jesus" in scripture. One of the things I appreciate when the Holy Spirit is referred to with female pronouns is the way that reference can attend to the work—physical, emotional, and administrative—of women and especially mothers, often just as hidden, inexplicable, and unappreciated as Hers. The "work" of building relationships, seeking reconciliation, promoting resiliency, and doggedly insisting on each person's unconditional worth despite our differences is as essential today as in biblical times, but maybe we can start there, with God's ministry of overlooked details. Before the Holy Spirit is named, there are books of the Bible where God is not even mentioned. Why are they even in the Bible?

In the book of Ruth, Naomi and her daughters-in-law navigate around other relationships (with Naomi's sons, who die) on the way to claiming or rejecting their relationships with one another. Orpah leaves them, but Ruth steadfastly refuses to go away, choosing instead to take care of Naomi. Ruth does what needs to be done to provide them both protection, a family, and a future by initiating relationship with Boaz. Their offspring are part of the lineage of Jesus, but when we wonder where God is in this story, we need look no further than the title character, Ruth. God does these things too, the things that need to be done to make a way for us and our people after death upends what we had known about our future. God chooses foolishly to love us not only with words of promise but concrete actions that move us into abundant life once more. God does these ridiculous things, like a soon-to-be sandwich generation daughter-in-law who claims her own power and makes a home where she is, for everybody's sake.

In the book of Esther, God is not explicitly part of the action either. Esther is an orphan raised by her cousin Mordecai, part of the Jewish minority in the kingdom of Persia. When the king's first wife Vashti defies his command, there is an opening for a new queen. Esther, who had entered the king's harem because of her beauty, is chosen. She finds herself in a position that is simultaneously subservient, dangerous, and powerful. I propose that these same adjectives describe what it is like to put ourselves in close proximity to God, as a pastoral leader. Esther, alone in the world, is persuaded by Mordecai to speak up to the king for the Jewish people, against whom a genocide is planned, despite the potential consequences to herself. Perhaps it is "for just such a time as this" (Es. 4:14) that she has risen to prominence, to get beyond herself and put the well-being of others first. There is something Godly in there, for sure. It is the individual's job to use whatever privilege they have been given to protect others who are at risk.

Airing our grievances is certainly valid and necessary within relationships. Consider the parts of scripture where communities and individuals raise their complaints to God: Lamentations, Psalms, Job, and many of the major and minor prophets. In our human relationships, when things are not going well, we need to hear it. There is a way to do this that preserves our relationships better than other means—addressing complaints directly and appropriately. Remember that Jesus instructed, "If another member of the church sins against you, go and point out the fault when the two of you are alone. If the member listens to you, you have regained that one. But if you are not listened to, take one or two others along with you, so that every word may be confirmed by the evidence of two or three witnesses" (Matt. 18:15–16). This does not include hitting "reply all" to criticize in an e-mail thread or bringing up criticism at announcement time or at an annual meeting. Our "church family" needs actively to teach our members how to address complaints face-to-face in appropriate circumstances. The risk of never talking about how we hurt or disappoint each other could be that we would never get better at nurturing our relationships. I have no illusions that we will ever stop hurting one another, but we might at least recognize when we are doing so and speak up when others hurt us.

I have served as a part-time interim pastor for four congregations at the time of writing this, some of them while having no childcare beyond my younger daughter's two-and-a-half hours of preschool and the iffy one-hour afternoon nap. So we minimized my role. I preached each week, presided at communion, and led funerals. Besides meeting with families at the time of a death, those are the most visible tasks of a pastor. If these are all we do, many people will perceive the congregation has a pastor. What else is there? Could not a congregation "survive" like this, with guest preachers?

Like a swimming duck, who seems serene above the water but who is kicking constantly underneath, she will never move forward without that underwater propeller. We are all constantly changing and our faith needs translating into our ever-evolving lives. To move forward as a congregation along with the world around us and respond with a nurtured and engaged faith to the changing needs of those inside and outside of the church, we cannot simply stand still. As any parent who has tried to get children out of the door for school knows, we will not get ready and go in any kind of timely manner unless someone is repeatedly coaching us, reminding us, and *making* us move. Yet we only follow when we trust the leader, and building that relationship takes time, especially for those of us who have had our trust broken in the past.

As an interim, I have preached the funerals of many mothers and grandmothers before realizing that I could preach with great authority on their mothering behaviors and the mothering of God, even when I did not know the women themselves. In my conversations with families, I searched for the deceased's most notable characteristic, so we could bond over that and hear the good news of hope through it. Yet for a mother who did a thousand unnoticed actions every day of her children's or grandchildren's or great-grandchildren's lives, there is not just one notable quality. We do not know the half of what she did for us. Yet all the mothering adds up to constancy, support, and a confidence to go out and come back home knowing we are loved.

Now, all mothers fail sometimes; we are not saints, and we do not have to canonize a mother in order to appreciate that she let her life and her identity be shaped by her relationships with her children. God, too, is shaped by relationship with us. Love makes mothers do things we never thought we would do and brings highs and lows of joy and fear and unfathomable love and anger. We have been in this together, parents and children, and God continues in it with us, too.

The church women preparing the funeral luncheon often have stories to tell about the beloved departed mothers too. They are the engine that runs most churches. How long have we overlooked or ignored the ways the "church mothers" have cared for all the details for our congregations? In the majority–West African congregation I served, there was a desire to make a big deal about Mother's Day. The observance is not a religious holiday and can be painful for those who have struggled with fertility, mothers or children who are estranged, or those whose mothers or children have died. One thing I appreciated about the congregation, however, was the honoring of all women of a certain age as the "mothers of the church." Some of the oldest generation were white women and some were matriarchs from the Liberian community. The testimony was true: these women mother our church. They polish the pews, take care of the meals we share, wash the altar cloths, keep the children in line, notice who is absent and organize meal delivery when a family is struggling. They mother us, alongside and in conjunction with the pastor.

At other times, instead of going unnoticed, my mothering provokes stares. Walking the halls of a hospital, nursing home, or drug store wearing my clergy collar turns some heads. People feel compelled to comment: "Are you a priest? A nun?" (Or if they notice I am pregnant, or I have my children with me, their eyes widen and eyebrows raise.) "What are you?!" While their ignorance seems quaint on the one hand, it is also a call to action. It is part of my job to walk around in public, blowing people's minds by being a clergy mother, modeling the hashtag #thisiswhatapastorlookslike. Even for those of us who do not wear clergy-specific clothing regularly, civic settings are the place to break it out: while accompanying people to court, testifying at city hall, or being part of the crowd at protests, rallies, or press conferences for community organizing. I am also not beyond bringing my children along to such actions to draw attention and give a certain impression. The stance I embody is a paradox to some people—a professional church leader and white woman with children in tow is invested in immigrant human rights? My body showing up casts doubt on the false claim that we are divided by clear lines; I will intentionally dress to look like a pastor in public if I think it can pry open people's minds or faith just a little bit.

Chance encounters do not have nearly the impact of sustained trusting relationships; however, seeing someone like me doing my job tells young girls (and others) that ministry leadership is a possibility for all who are called by God. People who worship in churches where women are prohibited from leading need to see us going about our normal lives. We are mothering, something that is likely very familiar to women whose social parameters are limited to that role, as well as preaching, teaching, and equipping the saints. Social media not only allows us to connect with each other, but also to interact with those who think the church is a monolithic, anti-feminist institution. We are a key part of how God cares for and works in the world. And we are mothers.

QUESTIONS FOR REFLECTION

Clergy Women:

1. How do you currently process feedback related to your parenting or leadership in the congregation?

2. Can you share a time when you or your family were the "case study" for a congregation on any issue, and how it went?

3. What do you see as the risks of naming publicly the conflicts between our parent and pastor roles? What might be the benefits of being honest about the struggle?

Support System:

1. If you are a PK yourself, what are your biggest impressions of life in that "public" family?

2. What behind-the-scenes actions of God are most meaningful to you? Where have you noticed those actions in scripture or your own life?

3. Has your congregation's woman pastor or mothering pastor ever come up in conversation away from the church? What did you say about her leadership?

~~

CHAPTER 5

God Give Us Discipline . . . and Flexibility

We wondered in chapter one if God started mothering by responding to Adam and Eve's defiance. Developing an approach to discipline (for our own and others' actions) is by no means a linear process, because all parents vacillate between responding with love and firmness or reacting out of our own exasperation. We may try a different tactic, because what worked in one relationship does not work in another, or we realize something about ourselves revealed by that approach. People of faith have drawn different pictures of God's discipline throughout scripture. When God abandons one course of action to guide humanity in favor of another, it is not always clear whether it is because the method of discipline did not bring about the desired result or because, effective though it was, it was not how God wanted to relate to her children.

Methods of Discipline

Ultimatums do not work, at least as a method of discipline. They may scare another into doing what we want occasionally. Threats of punishment may be motivators to action for a specific leader (for example, the threat to Esther that if she did not speak up, she and her family would perish). If the point is to raise a person who knows they are loved and so can love others, threats and punishments do not get us there. Discipline goes both directions, indicating a relationship between those with different levels of power.

When we read the flood story in Genesis, do we characterize God as wiping out those who were wicked so that the remnant will be scared into obedience? What else could be going on? Following the flood story, Noah and his offspring are busy proving they have learned nothing. Noah's sons shame him by reporting his drunken nakedness to each other, while Noah's daughters take turns getting him drunk so he will impregnate them. The flood did not rid the world of that horrible habit people have of objectifying each other. Yet God promised never to do this again, setting limits on Godself. "I will never again wipe out the living things upon the earth," God vowed, and made the rainbow the symbol of that promise. Perhaps God came to the conclusion that this is not how God wants to relate to humankind, regardless of their actions. God's response, as the immensely more powerful one in our relationship, becomes self-disciplined in making a way forward with humanity.

God's judgment can be swift and fierce. God reacts to the idolatrous Israelites at the foot of Mount Horeb when Moses returns, bringing the commandments to people who are already breaking them. God creates order for them as a way to define their relationship with God, because "I am the Lord your God who brought you out of Egypt" (Ex. 20:2). Therefore, you shall relate to me and each other in these ways. Before the commandments are even delivered, the people have pooled their jewelry to make a golden calf idol. This is not going to go well. However, as the Israelites grew into their identity as children of the Lord God, those commandments became defining, not something imposed upon them; the commandments had become a means of understanding who they were as people. This is not a system of threats and punishments, but a portrait of our relationship, and the discipline that maintains it.

Later, God sends a plague throughout the camp of Israel, when they had sexual relations with the women of Moab and bowed down to their gods. God reacts swiftly and decisively with wrath, and 24,000 died before it was over (Num. 25). To me, this feels like a moment of passionate reaction, a departure from any planned strategy of discipline.

When I need my children to just do what I am asking *right now* because I have other things to deal with, I know that the hissed threat is not a long-term discipline strategy. I am not cultivating their self-regulation based on love for other human beings. It can feel as if we are all coming off the adrenaline of a battle, and I just need no screaming or running around so I can talk to someone about a serious matter. I can hear in my own words that this moment is about my needs and not their development. At other times I reinforce that I am going to love them no matter what. Yet there are those situations in which the only way to command their full attention in public and achieve immediate compliance is to use a serious tone. So, I bribe or threaten. I know in the moment that it is merely a stopgap measure. I also know I will need to do some work in a quiet moment later, about how and why I need my kids to behave differently in the future. If I want them to integrate these behaviors (not interrupting adults in serious conversation), then a commandment alone is not going to do it, nor is practicing self-discipline myself; we will need to reinforce how it is part of who we are in a myriad of different ways, later.

My two daughters have very different personalities, so I find myself responding differently to them. The one who demands more attention, and immediate responses meeting her very specific expectations, gets more. So it can be with church folks. Many congregations have an instigator, a nemesis for the pastor who takes up a larger proportion of the pastor's emotional energy. When we consider the main characters in the narrative of the Bible, I wonder, for all of the beloved drama-creating Moseses and Davids and Pauls, how all the children of God unnamed or barely mentioned in scripture taught and changed God's parenting over the millennia? Our more flexible, adaptable daughter surprises me, especially when she shows us suddenly a skill I think I have neglected to practice enough with her. Even the one who is not the "squeaky wheel" learns and grows from our less intentional parenting. This kind of subtle influence comforts me when I know I am spending too much time with particular church members. A recent study reported the positive influence on self-esteem in young women who grew up seeing female pastors in leadership, regardless of whether they went into ministry themselves. This makes me hopeful that even if we can't remember each other by name, perhaps my presence may have been part of some young women's unconscious formation.

God becoming human through Jesus creates an enduring relationship with more of humanity. Notice whom this approach has reached: primarily Gentiles, those "all nations" whom Abraham's progeny was to bless. Unfortunately, the things Christians have done in the name of Christ to hurt others—from the Crusades to the present day—have sabotaged this loving embrace of God. Yet perhaps the parenting method we might see in the incarnation was intentional. Instead of sending children away from us to a "time out" when they break the rules, we are now invited to calm both of our reactions with a "time in": to embrace, hold tight, and bring down all of our racing heart rates with closeness. God chose this approach, embodied in the human person of Jesus. The law and prophets are not replaced, but "fulfilled" (Matt. 5:17) when God physically entered the fray, embracing all kinds of hurting people. Jesus left in his wake the Holy Spirit, that force of inspiration for forgiveness and speaking the language of others (as at Pentecost). Jesus proclaimed a new kind of relationship with the God who is still speaking through and to us. God is in the interactions between us. That inspires me to make my own actions intentional instead of reactionary. It makes me want to act with more maturity. What if we prized this parenting method of getting closer as the most significant way God interacts today? It has more potential to change our hearts and interactions with others than the threat of punishment or alienation could.

What effect could reflecting upon this parenting method of God have on congregational life? Perhaps we would let go of our need to manage others' behavior and look instead for ways to get closer to them. Whether they behave how we want them to, we will be closer, and that is the point. How can we build deeper relationships with those teenagers or young adults who have pulled away from our faith community (instead of judging them or their families for not meeting our expectations)? How can we reconcile with the folks who live in our church building's neighborhood but because of a long history of our rules or judgment, cannot see us as family? If we truly want to get closer, it will need to be with the kind of vulnerability God took on in becoming human.

One parenting behavior we rarely acknowledge, but God models from Abraham on, is being changed through bargaining. Parenting is nearly constant bargaining. Abraham bargains to preserve the cities of Sodom and Gomorrah if even ten righteous men can be found in them. One might say God invites this. Before announcing the intention to destroy these wicked cities, we hear a piece of God's inner monologue:

> Shall I hide from Abraham what I am about to do, seeing that Abraham shall become a great and mighty nation, and all the nations of the earth shall be blessed in him? No, for I have chosen him, that he may charge his children and his household after him to keep the way of righteousness and justice.
>
> Gen. 18:18–19

Should a parent eliminate the conversation and act, or for the sake of instruction and cultivating leadership, engage in discussion? God chooses the latter in this case. It turns into a negotiation. In Exodus, God tells Moses of the inclination to wipe out the whining, ungrateful Israelites and start over. By saying it before doing it, God is inviting intervention. God allows Moses to negotiate down the punishment. Moses negotiates between parent and children (Ex. 32:14;

Num. 14:12). To witness God being talked out of this motherly anger makes the God-as-parent metaphor more real to me, not less.

My all-time favorite biblical story of God bargaining and being changed by interaction is Jesus and the Canaanite woman. Jesus has clear rules and boundaries for his own attention and healing power in Matthew 15:21–28 (or another version in Mark 7:25–30). He tries to ignore the woman crying out to him, sending her away with a clear statement:

> "I was sent only to the lost sheep of the house of Israel." But she came and knelt before him, saying, "Lord, help me." He answered, "It is not fair to take the children's food and throw it to the dogs." She said, "Yes, Lord, yet even the dogs eat the crumbs that fall down from their masters' table." Then Jesus answered her, "Woman, great is your faith! Let it be done for you as you wish." And her daughter was healed instantly.

Jesus allows his heart to be moved. He—fully human and fully divine—changes who he will care about and how he will act, based on interacting with this mother. Perhaps he admires her perseverance, her faith not only that God can heal her child but that she can argue God's own son into doing so. Never underestimate the power of a mother's drive to protect or heal her children; it is of Godly proportions. Perhaps what changed Jesus's mind was hearing her repeat the word he had used for this mother and child: "dogs." That word calls Jesus to account about who he is and what he is on this earth to do. Is his purpose to dehumanize some of God's children, or to express God's unconditional love for each and every one of them? The give-and-take of negotiating with the Lord God or Jesus is partly about advocating on our own behalf, but also partly reminding them of who they are in relation to us. To love like a parent means being open to changing our minds or actions in relationship with our children. Who better to deliver that reminder to God than a mother?

Beginning with Abraham and Sarah, becoming God's particular chosen ones has meant leaving an old identity and people behind. This was also true of those prominent citizens forced into the Assyrian and Babylonian exiles. My mom did this when I was nine years old, putting me on an airplane to spend three summer weeks with my grandmother in Wyoming. In the thirty years since, my mother has repeatedly joked that she thinks she overdid "the independence thing" in raising me. Jesus himself describes the necessity of his disciples leaving behind their mothers, fathers, brothers, and sisters to follow him. Sometimes he is quite harsh. There are many things to talk about with all of those stories but squint your eyes and view it through the lens of a parenting God, and all three situations testify to the same themes. We mature as God's children when we are pushed out of our comfort zones, often becoming a minority faction. Children of God become more independent by stepping out in faith, making decisions without the culture around us reinforcing that identity. That call of God or commandment to "follow me" away from our familial identities is for our own good, and remarkably makes us better equipped to lead. There will certainly be growing pains. Parents know that striking out on their own is the only way children can try out their independence, test the boundaries, and determine how they will relate to others based on what they have learned.

Respect of the Office Is for Women, Too

"Would you say that to a male pastor?" When a clergywoman is compelled to ask that question, the answer is almost always "no." Clergywomen must draw boundaries in order to keep sexism at bay. We are called to this disciplinary work within the church. We just did not know how much of our ministry this task of responding to sexism could take up.

The authority Jesus earned and therefore the authority he gave to his evangelists and disciples was relational. Anyone is Jesus's brother or sister or mother if they are seeking to know and do the will of God. To lead a particular faith community, we must be committed to that identity, following the discernment path established by the church. A pastor's authority comes from being properly called, examined, and approved by the institution as ordination rites state. Our authority is not rooted in resembling the clergymen of people's childhoods, or the societal assumption that a deep voice or looming male presence "just carries authority." Clergy women embody the authority, even when disconcerting to some, of faithful leadership. Yet we know that productive unsettling requires finesse to move beyond defensiveness and make change possible. Seeking and doing the will of God can require convincing, guiding, and mothering.

A colleague addressed an older man in her congregation who has repeatedly undermined her, telling him, "I have noticed that the only times you engage with or comment upon my sermons are when you wish to correct an error. I invite you to reflect on that." The existence of clergy women invites people to reflect on even their internalized gender stereotypes and attitudes. Naming the unequal expectations aimed at women clergy is the first step. We are often expected to perform both the role of pastor and functions that in days of yore were fulfilled by the pastor's wife. Female clergy should not be expected both to prepare the sermon and bring a pie for the potluck after service, or to host a staff party during Advent. We may have to define what never was defined before: that an employee cannot also volunteer at the church. If my contract is part-time, for twenty hours a week, I will not "volunteer" ten additional hours to set up the women's circle rummage sale as if I am a member volunteering. I am the only one who can provide the clarity that attending "family camp" does not count as vacation time for me. Setting these boundaries may not feel good to me but doing so is a key part of my role.

Sexism may show up in starkest relief when we work with a male pastoral colleague. If the male colleague is addressed as Pastor His-Last-Name, then why is the female pastor called by her first name with no title? Do people talk about her children, but few ever think to mention her male colleague's children in conversations about church matters? Would anybody ever comment on how his new haircut makes him look sexy or remind him about his weight at a potluck? Is it appropriate to address him with a nickname equivalent to "Little Mama"? Women clergy have heard all of these things. Erin Wathen roots out the depth of sexism in the church and our lived theology in her bestselling book *Resist and Persist: Faith and the Fight for Equality* (2018). Sexism has no place in the body of Christ, but it certainly has a foothold in our churches.

In addition to challenging stereotypes of women and leadership, clergy women who are also mothers may need to sort through some additional psychological responses. Male clergy also experience associations with congregants' own fathers, perhaps heightened by using the title Father for clergy in some traditions. Yet something feels different about the emotional intimacy associated with letting down our guard around Mother like with no one else, seeping into our relationship with a pastor who also mothers. Everyone has a relationship with their mother, or feelings around the absence of that relationship. These are strong feelings, primal to our identities, and can emerge as transference onto a mother figure. Women clergy must analyze every relationship to maintain the boundaries of caregiver professional. We know that if we do not hold firm, greater damage may be caused to those who are emotionally vulnerable. The meeting where I have to make these boundaries clear is going to be painful, but it is better to have it earlier than later. We may invite people to reflect on how and where to nurture the close relationship they seem to be yearning for, but which we cannot fill. Maybe we can talk about what it is like to no longer be mothered, but to seek out solidarity instead.

Especially in church bodies where bishops are elected, whom we choose is a statement about our values. It cannot be only those women who have waited until their children were self-sufficient, or those who did not have children, who demonstrate significant leadership ability. I would love to see how women leaders in the thick of parenting could actually influence or change the expectations we have of our leaders. Bishop Kristen Kuempel of the Northwest Intermountain Synod of the ELCA has been honest on social media that sometimes being a bishop and mother looks like answering synod e-mails from the pediatrician's waiting room. Depending on the denomination and its polity, bishops have the opportunity to hold firm on ruling on calls or appointments to certain positions, and when to make exceptions. I have yet to hear anyone compare those decisions to the personal boundaries around our lives as clergy mothers or the firm boundaries yet flexible mercy of a mothering God.

The most difficult boundaries to create and hold steady are around what we let affect us emotionally. Will I let the toxic interactions with a parishioner or staff member keep me up at night? Will I let a disparaging voice echo in my head, distracting me from being confident in my interactions? Will I bring injuries or grief home with me?

At least clergy mothers know, because one part of our lives informs the other: boundaries are key (and not always appreciated). Clergy mothers set boundaries at church around our time, energy, and effort so we have something to offer at home. We set boundaries at home if we are to faithfully serve a congregation. We must carve out time away from both church and family to remember who we are, and delight in that, or we show up weary and bitter in all our settings. Self-disclosure about our own struggles can be turned against us if it is cited as compromising our leadership. Yet sharing our struggles can also humanize us, making us accessible and relatable to others. We are all trying to love our people, and some of our efforts succeed better than others. I find that accountability with others gives me permission or a push to set limits on what I can do. The mom-guilt is real. The pastor-guilt is real. But perhaps grace is also the truest it has ever been, since we need it all the time?

System-Wide Boundaries

I appreciate that on the seventh day of creation, God rested. Imagine that, clergy mothers, not only a full night of sleep, but an entire twenty-four hours to rest. That would be very good indeed. We are commanded to take a weekly Sabbath to honor God and the God-image in us. God rested after creating. So too, parents who adopt, foster, or birth children into the world need a sacred time set aside at the end of the creation of our family to rest and to be in awe, in order to be able to identify how very good it is to have our lives and identities turned inside out. Also, we desperately need sleep.

I need sleep more than the average adult, I think. Our older daughter came to us as a two-and-a-half-year-old champion sleeper. She could nap on trains, planes, or in automobiles. She was an early riser, though; I practically leaped out of bed at the first sound of movement every morning, but maybe that was because one time I came into the kitchen and found her playfully fumbling with the knobs on the stove. We put up child gates shortly after that. When I gave birth to our second child, the sleep deprivation became a true risk. I could not do this on my own. My spouse had to step between us in our bedtime ritual, and I had to endure thinking how, from the indignant cries, she must hate me. Please save any parenting criticism for the comments of a parenting blog. My point here is that we were both caught in a cycle that we needed external help and structure to escape.

What has been true for me in claiming Sabbath as a pastor-mother is this: Unless others around me are also invested in me having rest, a sacred day off, or parental leave, I cannot make it happen. Congregations with clergy who are fathers may not have this conversation as often, but once again the existence of clergy mothers makes it a necessity. Amidst the admonishments to prioritize self-care that lay the burden squarely on the individual, we must instigate conversations about the number of evening meetings that take us away from our families, how and when vacation must be taken with school schedules (which can coincide with Christmas and Easter), and the necessary length of parental leave for bonding and recovery when we add a new family member.

Clergy mothers have the authority to claim the boundaries we need around our own time, energy, and emotional investment, but also to fight for others to be able to do the same. We need to advocate for each other, especially because when we are in the thick of things—like sleep deprivation—we cannot always clearly advocate for our own needs. I will not tolerate older generations of church women shaming mothers with young children for not running the church in addition to their households. I can establish policies so that the next pastor in any congregation I serve will have guaranteed substantial parental leave. I can make a powerful case from experience and theology that our members should be pushing at the state capital for guaranteed earned sick and safe time for all employees. We do not need self-soothing like bubble baths or chocolates, but communal responsibility for nurturing our families. Think of how this good news could be heard by our church's neighbors. God is like a parent, more invested in relationships than financial productivity, and so is our church. Would it give us permission to spend more time listening and less time competing for attention? If God is open to being changed by interacting with us, then we, too, could make it a defining part of our identity that we are "works in progress," ready to be shaped by our neighbors' stories and needs. We have non-negotiable boundaries, but they all revolve around our commitment to making sure everyone knows we are all unconditionally beloved children of God.

QUESTIONS FOR REFLECTION

Clergy Women:

1. Consider a time when you have changed your mind or the "rules" for the sake of caregiving. With the benefit of hindsight, would you do it all over again?

2. How do you teach about sexism, ageism, and other discrimination you face, in ways people can hear and integrate into their understanding?

3. Which have been the hardest boundaries for you to hold, either with your family or your congregation? Why do you think that is so?

Support System:

1. How has bargaining with children or others for whom you are a caregiver changed your methods of discipline or made you understand your role differently?

2. What might recognizing God's flexibility and changing strategies for discipline mean to your own parenting?

3. How have you supported healthy boundaries for others: coworkers, other parents, church leaders, and so forth? To whom do you give credit for helping protect your time, energy, and effort from overextension?

CHAPTER 6

Divided Attention and Loyalty

In my mind's eye, mothering and teaching are inextricably intertwined; this may be because my mother is an early childhood teacher. My brothers and I watched our mom cut out thousands of shapes for crafts over the course of our childhood, and purchase millions of stickers. She would pull out different picture books, organized according to holidays or seasons, whenever we turned the calendar. We could playfully imitate her "teacher voice," as distinct from her "mom voice," and this English major can trace my love of language back to having a teacher-mother who was always putting books in our hands. When my older brother and I were under five, Mom ran a play group in our finished basement for all the neighborhood kids around our ages. Our playroom was literally our classroom. Later she worked in preschools and when our younger brother went to elementary school, Mom returned to work closer to full-time. We were her first priority, but we also knew that she had a very important role outside of taking care of us. That was a valuable seed to plant in our young minds. Our mother always had another part of her identity, and people other than us to consider. Now that my parents are "empty nesters," my mother's volunteering revolves around her teaching pursuits.

None of us are one-dimensional. Our teachers do not live at the school—as kindergartners may believe—nor do our pastors live at the church. We should not have to hide one role to step into another. The tension between our multiple callings may even be faithful, reflecting the image of God in us, and perhaps challenging us to become better at all of them. As persons of faith, relatives, friends, neighbors, students, or employees, we all have parts of our identity to balance and blend together. "Father, Son, and Holy Spirit" or "Creator, Redeemer, and Sanctifier" are some of our human attempts at describing how God's actions are divided yet always connected. Somehow, God does not stop being one member of the Trinity to also be fully present in another one of the three. The different persons of the Trinity are in relationship with each other, perhaps in tension, but also supporting and strengthening the others. If only we could appreciate the divided attention required by our multiple roles.

It Is Good for the Pastor

The pastors I know who have lasted in parish ministry are those who have a ministerial identity outside of caring for their parish. Congregations benefit from the stability of their sustained leadership and the ongoing renewal provided by this outside ministry.

I know pastors of congregations who work on a team in college campus ministries or run some kind of demographic fellowship group (such as for adoptive families or queer young adults). One dear friend is a parish priest and also a marriage and family counselor. There are those who present workshops, keynote at conferences, or consult in their areas of expertise. My circle of clergy-writer colleagues is ever-expanding, giving us life by using our artistic and teaching skills. It all helps. Burnout is a looming threat when congregations or denominations are declining and the only ministry identity clergy have is within the congregation. A congregation's failure to thrive can feel like our own failure, when really that abundant life depends on many factors. We need divided attention and loyalty to know that the "family systems" we tend are not our only identity. They are certainly important, central even, but not all that defines us.

When I was a pastoral intern in a five-point parish in rural northeast Montana, my supervising pastor encouraged me to embrace the role of "community pastor" for the small town where I lived in the parsonage that year. I officiated for all the funerals at the church next door to my residence, attended sporting events, and ate at all the community fundraisers. At the time I was twenty-five years old and single; in other words, I was practically alone in several demographics in that community. Although my stay there had a scheduled end, it influenced my choices afterward significantly. As I was trying out the role of pastor, I sensed that I was always a supporting actor in the drama of other people's lives, and I wanted to have my own plotline. I hoped not only to preside at other people's weddings, baptisms, confirmations, and other milestones, but to find a partner to share my life with and create my own family. These priorities influenced where I requested my first call assignment after seminary graduation. I knew I would be dissatisfied if "pastor" was my only or overriding identity.

There is not unlimited time, of course. To carve out time for an artistic endeavor, activism, or consulting work that sustains us in ministry is untenable in certain seasons of our lives. Tending our relationships, especially parenting, may take much of our non-ministry time and mental space. In bi-vocational settings, financial pressures may demand that we find unrelated part-time work for the income. Ministry demands can expand to fill the time allotted if we let them. When we have the time to breathe, though, we feel the ache from missing who we have been besides mothers and priests. What are our other joys? What else feeds our souls to create, or touches others when we share our gifts? Creativity should not be reserved for the privileged few, but a guarded and valued part of the pastoral role. It is a power that can sustain all of us and should be valued as part of the public identity of any pastor. When the congregation was the center of civic life, the pastor's public role was part of the job description. It can be again, but instead of praying at local sporting events or Rotary breakfasts perhaps we can create our own public contributions according to our passions or the needs we perceive around us.

When I wrote about this topic for my denomination's online magazine, I noted that having a sense of vocation and identity beyond the bounds of the parish also enables us to leave a congregation well, when it is the appropriate time, and to stay gone for the benefit of the next pastoral leader. It is painfully difficult to retire if your entire identity revolves around a congregation. As a bishop's associate described it to me, pastors need to learn that we are really amphibious, but if we never get out of the water, we will not discover that we can actually breathe in the air. Clergy mothers, for whom the parish could never be our sole focus, have some survival skills to teach our colleagues. Pastors cannot expect to find all our needs met in congregational ministry, or we will never let them outgrow us.

It Is Good for the Congregation

There are certainly times when those in our care need our undivided attention. Especially if they have had their trust broken before, people need clarity about who will be there for them in their need, without unintentional confusion. My children always get my exclusive attention when they are sick or injured. Similarly, when a congregation sells their building, faces the death of a well-loved member, or confronts another major transition, it is a season when the pastor's full attention is needed. Someday, they will no longer be sifting through the end of what had previously been known and trusted, and instead starting to grow anew. How does a pastor recognize when it is time to encourage independence again? How does a mother? Women pastors serve more often in smaller, financially strapped congregations that make bivocational ministry necessary for income, so we will likely be on the front lines of this shift.

How do we listen to a congregation that is grieving because it can no longer afford a full-time pastor, but then empower them to use that circumstance as part of their witness? Having divided attention ourselves begins the process. We can testify: divided attention causes strain, but also creates different models of ministry.

If a clergy mother modeling this split attention, or perhaps a pastor who also writes books, presents workshops, or teaches at the local community college, feels like a risk to congregations, that perception may be well founded. The greatest positive risk is that congregation members will be stretched into more independent, faithful adults, actively ministering themselves. The entire congregation will need more than milk, as Paul says, but real food to engage with their faith and take action themselves. A congregation's reticence to become the caregivers instead of being cared for can be worn away, as many are empowered to take the congregation's ministries into their own hands. Clergy mothers prepare the church—against its will, sometimes—to step into the authentic, participatory role of being Christian community in the world. Sometimes the greatest empowerment is in making space for lay people to do things themselves.

As a pastor and mother, I intentionally let things go if they do not have the support we need to attempt them. It is okay if Bible school doesn't happen this year, but it does not feel okay. It is painful when a clergy mother does not make it happen by sheer force of will, but everybody else feels the lesson. What happens if we do not have the volunteers to pull off an event? Then we recognize that a pastor in the office does not actually make us a church. Everyone's participation is needed for that.

Self-aware clergy are vital to this brave new world of reinventing church. However, not every pastor, just like not every mother, functions as if our role is to work ourselves out of a job by equipping those in our family to minister to one another and the world. Usually unexamined, our complicated motivations for taking on these roles could include a hunger for the attention we think we will receive from being the mother or the pastor, or a yearning to be loved ourselves. Perhaps we are seeking a direction for our lives or a way to exercise authority. Even when we genuinely begin with a sense of calling from God, our purpose can get muddled along the way. Sometimes both mothers and clergy stand in the way of our family's or congregation members' independence, by making everything go through us. The longer we are in a congregation, the more common this tends to be among pastors. We might become resentful if decisions are made without our approval and will not champion ideas that are not our own. We could prolong dependence by bringing up our past sacrifices or discourage questions or new thinking. Newcomers to the family system have to fit into the patterns we prescribe or remain as outsiders, when we are unwilling to adapt to their contributions.

What seems a worthy parenting goal, especially among immigrants, is "to give the next generation opportunities we did not have." As a pastor in a denomination of immigrants where that identity is still significant—primarily German or Scandinavian—I see programming designed for those who wanted to preserve their language or traditions is not relevant several generations later. Giving our children everything does not necessarily mean they will want to keep it.

One parenting strategy for developing responsibility is to start with tasks a child thinks are fun, and encourage ownership of those jobs. Never let on that sweeping is actually a chore. Praise how well they do it, but also the passion or perseverance that keeps them working on it. A single young woman in my first congregation, my only peer at the time, attended sporadically. When I helped create a "Here, Near, and Far" team for social justice/mission activities, I identified the similar priorities we shared and hoped that the team would be a way for her to invest, while providing needed leadership for a new initiative. "Thank you so much for putting your effort into keeping this in front of these folks who, let's face it, have an abundance to share," I framed the task. I convinced her to spearhead one of the initiatives, and she (a teacher) ended up connecting the congregation with a boarding school in Malawi through our companion synod. This friend continues to support and lead ministries in the congregation after I moved away.

We might align our efforts to empower and share responsibility for the ministries of our congregations with Martin Luther's theology of a "priesthood of all believers." We are all participants in God's action in the world; lay people are not of secondary importance in seeking out and expressing God's will. Explaining this concept aloud keeps the pastor accountable, because the words will lose their meaning if we do not follow through. The idea of a universal priesthood draws upon Exodus 19:6; Isaiah 61:6, and 1 Peter 2:5. We might also hear it from Genesis 2 (dominion), the Great Commission (Matt. 28), or the reciprocity of the early church that held everything in common and divided jobs among themselves (Acts 2). The church communities to whom Paul wrote the letters that form much of the New Testament certainly did not operate as if spreading the gospel was Paul's job alone. In other words, sharing the responsibility and joy of ministry—being church—is an oft-repeated biblical concept.

The office of pastor exists for the sake of church order. Any Christian *could* preach the gospel, baptize, or share communion. Yet for the sake of church order, and to head off at the pass those who would do so for their own gain or in a way that obscures Christ, we set those things aside for those ordained to Word and Sacrament. I think it is meant to keep these gifts from becoming overtaken by our egos, but certainly not to keep the laity from doing ministry or being the body of Christ. It is the responsibility and privilege of each one of us to get to know each other, visit, notice absences, and organize for particular care needs. Each of us can study, teach, pray, and apply scripture to how we will respond in the world. Certainly, it is for each of us to notice when a certain practice of our community excludes others.

In a 2019 piece published on youngclergywomen.org, Pastor Stephanie Sorge describes the double entendre of the "pastoral care team" when a new leader asked her whether that team provides pastoral care to the congregation, or to the pastor? It can be both: lay leaders can share the care load and consider the pastor and her family as members of the faith community that also need care. To put the burden on the mom or the pastor to ask for help means that we will inevitably wait until we are stretched almost beyond capacity before asking. If someone is actually watching out for us, they can catch the warning signs earlier. For example, a funeral on a Saturday when the pastor's spouse is out of town means that in addition to the family of the deceased needing support, the clergy mother might need people to show up to watch the kids or feed us when it is all said and done. The emotional drain of funerals is real.

When families or congregations function as if time is money, then the exorbitant investment of mothers' or pastors' time in caregiving never adds up because it is not easily quantifiable. "Being there" to build trust or studying in order to teach and guide our people well does not fit into a time sheet. We cannot log the minutes spent remembering the anniversary of a death, or an e-mail sent just to check in. The experimental work of building community in the midst of major cultural shifts is very different from the nuts and bolts work of running a building or institutional events and board structures. Mother-work is undervalued as much as the relational work of ministry can be.

What are the greatest benefits to children and congregations not being treated as the center of the universe? First, there is the glorious potential of communal responsibility for our family system, its actions, and its shared space. But I also wonder, are children in a family or members in a congregation, where divided attention or callings have become normative, actually less likely to act like gatekeepers? Do the boundaries around who is in the family/ congregation become more porous, or less discriminating? If we are accustomed to sharing clergy attention, does it establish a pattern of holding more lightly our ownership of our building, our public voice on behalf of those who are "outside" of us, or our identity beyond the heritage of the dominant group within our walls? I want to be hopeful for this. I know jealousy is real and shifting a family's or congregation's culture takes generations. I have heard parishioners say, "We will just outlast the pastor. When they leave, we will still be here and switch things back." But part of the great exodus of young adults from our congregations could very well be because when they went outside the church and discovered people worthy of their love, they would not return to a community that refuses to look outside, or live like they are part of all the "others" outside of their group. Young adulthood is a time when we discover that all families do not necessarily operate like ours, which leads to major assessment of what we want to take with us or leave behind.

Here is what I really want to know: If we are nurtured by mothers or pastors whose attention and focus we share with others, is our theology less likely to be exclusive? We inadvertently conflate pastors with God all the time, since we get most of our theology filtered through them. If they have concerns beyond us, meaningful work in the world alongside tending our needs, does that mean God does, too? A pastor involved in interfaith organizing work will find their preaching and interpretation of the ancient scriptures influenced by those relationships, right? A mother who is also a doctor or teacher or social worker or engineer is bound to have aspects of those careers seeping into her parenting. But the divided attention necessary to be a pastor-mother is itself a theological claim. This family or this congregation is not all that matters, to me or to God. Our relationship is not all God exists for. This subverts a hyper-personal faith that is only about me and Jesus. It is for the whole world that God became a heartbroken parent (and human child).

So, who are we, with our clearly limited view of God, to condemn any other human beings, created in the image of God? We do not have to consider ourselves God's exclusive focus to know that we are loved. The Bible not only leaves space for this, but Jesus preaches on it. "I have other sheep that do not belong to this fold" (John 10:16), he claims. In Luke 15, Jesus tells parables about caregivers who leave sheep, their household work, even the children still at home, to seek out the sheep, coin, or child who were lost. God is our ever-present mother, but a mother whose identity and calling beyond our family is to seek out and unconditionally love others.

This theology is possible. Opening up responsibility for ministry to the "priesthood of all believers" could change church life for the good. We need to discuss regularly why this is who we are and who God is calling us to be. It will be inexplicable to some why we should care about "outsiders" like refugees or LGBTQ people. What do those people have to do with us? It makes no sense, unless they are who God spends time with when we are not paying attention.

What Would It Look Like?

Becoming a congregation where the pastor balances parish life with another vocation (whether family relationships or another passion) may be a wake-up call to those who have never functioned this way. If the pastor has been tending myriad details nobody else seems to notice, people will indeed notice, and possibly resent it when that changes. If the pastor alone was calling people who hadn't been in worship in a while, like a mother remembering on behalf of the family to check in on relatives, it will not happen.

Given the similarities between pastoral ministry and mothering, it is not surprising that a majority of my examples have parallels in domestic labor. This is labor God does, too. Feeding, clothing, tending injuries, and soothing so that others can sleep are tasks God does in the form of the Lord God, Jesus, and the Holy Spirit.

When we share these daily tasks with others, perhaps there is more room for the Holy Spirit to move in our imaginations. God is concerned with multiplying the loaves and fishes, watching through the night, or interceding for us with sighs too deep for words, so there can be time for me to notice how God speaks and acts. With time and mental space for creativity, I can preach and teach and lead better. The solidarity of a God who can hold the details for me helps; giving them away to others in community so that I can turn my attention elsewhere is more life-giving still. What the Holy Spirit does within me, when I have time and space to ponder, is the soul-feeding inspiration for which I became a pastor. God leads me to surprising insights or angles of understanding scripture or a current situation.

If congregations built into their expectations not just uncluttered creative time for pastors preparing to preach and teach, but also time and attention for the other callings in their lives, what would that look like? To honor the split vocation that is parenting while ministering, childcare would need to be an integral part of any compensation package. I am thinking about parental leave, getting creative around evening meetings, and quality childcare during worship. These issues belong to all of us to solve. Can you imagine a church where summer programming gaps did not cause hours of childcare "calendar Tetris" for the clergy mother? Can you imagine a congregation where members take seriously their baptismal responsibility for the parish's children during worship? Does a congregation yet exist where a child's behavior is never going to prompt looks toward their parents, because every adult is involved in engaging kids in worship, not just squelching their childlike actions?

How can congregations see the values in clergy mother's divided loyalties? How can we, who are clergy mothers, shape an openness to shared attention? Will our congregations begin to note: "those of us who have no idea what that experience is like will learn so much from a clergy mother. What commitments might she bring for advocacy for parents and families? How will she hear God speaking through the scriptures because of her multiple roles?" This divided attention can be a gift. It is a gift to have someone whose calling it is to relate the word of God to our lives embody the balancing act between absorbing careers and caregiving in relationships. God blesses clergy mothers with divided attention and loyalty. It will bless us all.

QUESTIONS FOR REFLECTION

Clergy Mothers:

1. Which of your gifts do you dream about developing into a ministry when caring for children no longer takes so much of your attention?
2. Do you know of pastors or congregations who honor the leader's divided attention well? What does that look like?

Support Network:

1. What are some of your roles you consider a "calling"?
2. What experiences in your life helped you develop independence? What do you do to empower your own children's independence?
3. What are your remaining reservations about a pastor's attention being shared between the congregation and other callings?

CHAPTER 7

Emotional Labor

I could tell as soon as my husband started tussling with our younger daughter that this was not an episode the parents were going to win. Our three-year-old was trying to escape her row and chase me up to the chancel where I was leading worship. Greta had been okay sitting between her sister and dad for a while, but once I made contact with her during the sharing of the peace, I activated the mommy magnetism, and now she could not be anywhere other than with me without a tantrum. I was serving as an interim pastor at a congregation that worshiped at 5:00 p.m. on Saturdays out of necessity, since they used another congregation's building. That hour before dinner is one my mother referred to as "the witching hour" when we were kids, a hard time of day for self-regulation for children and parents alike. My husband and daughters had come along for worship since we had somewhere to go afterward; now the younger one was making me regret it. What is a clergy mother to do? I gave her a hug and tried to lead her back to Papa. I could feel my face getting hot. Greta crossed her arms across her chest and sat her body down on the step directly in front of the altar. I took a deep breath. The words of institution for Holy Communion that day would be delivered along with the glare of an indignant almost-three-year-old. Thankfully, the small gathering of people was good humored about walking past her scowl to receive the body and blood of Christ. At least she wasn't screaming. My heart rate slowed to normal after the benediction.

Embarrassment is an incredibly powerful emotion, up there with anger, joy, anxiety, and sadness. Mothers feel it hit hard.

Clergy mothers empathize with our children, react as their mothers, and also view events as we perceive a congregation experiences them. There are many perspectives to juggle before our own. We manage fallout for our own sake and to shape the congregation's culture, but to do so, we must hold all the feelings in the same armload. Part of our ministry and mothering will always be "emotional labor": the work of hiding our feelings or the projection of different emotions in order to lead pastorally. Emotional labor is a term coined by sociologist Arlie Russell Hochschild to describe how workers in service industries provide a positive customer experience by hiding their own feelings. Clergy are engaged in creating community where everyone can experience the unconditional love of God and pursue God's will together, not necessarily in making customers happy. Yet disguising our feelings sometimes comes with our mission.

Anxiety about the future is almost palpable in many mainline Protestant churches today. We are compelled by the hope we have in the gospel to preach hope. Yet we know that new life may require current practices of church to die before new forms of faith community take hold. It is an unresolvable tension to love the people we have, while deconstructing the institution they love. I am not subtle enough to introduce that news in a way people are glad to hear. Clergy have our own grief and perhaps anger to tend, and yet are called to preach resurrection hope and comfort those grieving the death of church as they know it. At least we have practice for this emotional labor from caregiving around the deaths and funerals of congregation members.

When a loved one is dying, someone should be there. Someone should wipe their chin, and respond to every muddled worry with assurance, patting their hand and telling them how dear they are. The memory care unit in nursing homes reminds me of mothering at the beginning of life. Visiting family members, pastors, and staff shepherd elders on that last part of the journey as we do children at the beginning: encouraging, touching, showering them with love although they know neither what is going on nor who they once were. All that matters is that they are loved now. We witness their decline as they perhaps witnessed our early development. When the time comes, we testify with our presence to the fact that they are beloved while dying, just as they have been in life. Sometimes those final moments are spent with family crowded around; for others, it is with one or two witnesses to the sacred moment. As a pastor, I have been the only visitor for an elder without family nearby, the second person in the room to support a dedicated caregiver, and the organizing presence to support a room full of people focused on their complicated tangle of relationships and feelings in the last moments with their loved one.

Officiating for the funeral or memorial service of someone I have never met is a very different experience emotionally than leading for someone I knew. I empathize with those who were close to the deceased and try to speak the hope of resurrection into their grief. When I also had a relationship with the one who died, I try to set my reactions aside to get through the service and find a different time and place to express my own feelings. I may be grieving a loving, supportive congregation member, or wrestling with my own relief and guilt over one who needed much. I might be fighting back the emotional reactions from ways the deceased resembled one of my family members, or myself. Yet I must lead, so I hide my own feelings. Similarly, most of us go into the ministry because we love the church and have found belonging there. It is painful to grieve the impending loss of the way church has been but see clearly that present patterns are not sustainable. We carry this grief but have to find safe spaces in which to process it.

Pastors and mothers get our feelings hurt, too. When my contributions are overlooked or misconstrued, I am just as likely to be angry or disappointed as anybody else. When the current state of the kitchen is taken for granted, but it took months or years of my sweat, anxiety, and effort to get it remodeled, I might admit to some bitterness. I did not labor in order to be applauded for it, but I am offended when credit is not given where it is due. In the biblical book of Ruth, Naomi is so bitter about the deaths of her sons and husband, her legacy, and her security that she tries to rename herself "bitter." One of her daughters-in-law leaves, but the other one stays with her. Ruth goes with the bitter older woman to her people's land and Ruth's solidarity means that Naomi also has a future. Yet even if we share our hurts publicly, they weigh us down, hunching our shoulders or stifling our joy. The solidarity of friends who stay with us even in our bitterness saves us.

Empathy

Emotional labor involves manipulation of the way we express our own feelings in order to influence others. Manipulation carries a negative connotation—but it may not always be a negative action. The ability to subtly shape and direct others' behaviors is both a talent and a necessity, dependent on emotional responses. Positive influencing is at the heart of raising children into responsible adults, and possibly also guiding a congregation to see and pursue God's vision beyond their own agendas. We must always call out abusive manipulation, but let us not underestimate the value of positive redirection, persuasion, and leveraging relationships for good. These are skills many mothers and clergy have developed in spades.

Of course, I want my kids and my parishioners to feel and do the "right" thing as I see it, but perhaps more simply I yearn for them to develop empathy. We can coach each other on what an empathetic response would be when we trust that we are each coming from a place of love. Our mutual goal is to empathize with each other and those who seem different from us, too. I hope those in my care will not only respond in this way during our time together, but after I am no longer around to notice. It seems like this is one of our essential tasks in raising children and overseeing faith communities. Where do we begin?

Sometimes parents find wielding guilt or enforcing gratitude to be effective in creating the behaviors we seek. On the surface, this seems to work in congregations, within cultures where pastors have great authority. After a major church-wide vote about the acceptance of LGBTQ clergy and same-sex marriage in my denomination, a Liberian matriarch in our half-immigrant congregation said, "When the missionaries from the United States came, they taught us this was not the way to be faithful. Now the leaders say it is okay. We followed them then, so I guess we can follow them now." Her argument was not to leave the denomination over the decision, but neither did this stance compel anyone to love or engage more deeply to understand their LGBTQ siblings. It was not a plea to be open to change for the sake of the other. I can recognize that although I have led in the church this way and parented this way, it is not a long-term strategy in either realm of leadership.

The alternative to enforcing behaviors with guilt might be modeling vulnerability and empathy. That is not what I did after the denominational vote of 2009, six months into my tenure at the congregation where half the parishioners were West African immigrants. I relied on the power of that church mother's advice to quell the audible displeasure. Others mentioned the power of the denomination over their congregation since they had received grants and more than their share of attention and effort from the bishop's office. The allegiance required of people who highly value loyalty convinced them to stay, yet the distrust of the institution did not go away; it just went underground. I manipulated in secret, inviting pastors to fill in during my vacation whom I knew identified as queer (but the congregation did not). Did I feel too new to the parish family to trust them or myself to engage in vulnerable dialogue about fears and change? I did not yet have children at home, so perhaps if I had already parented toddlers I would have recognized that parenting by declaration only works when they think you are watching. Adapting a behavior as their own only comes through repeated practice. I could have preached about my own struggles to understand or empathize with LGBTQ kin, when I did not think I knew anyone who identified as part of that community. This shifted dramatically for me when I worked at a church day camp in San Francisco that assertively affirmed same-sex couples as beloved and included.

Parenthood has taught me more courage than I was willing to muster back then, because more is obviously at stake. I have such influence over molding and shaping my children's worldviews, it is breathtaking. At their current ages, we might not have many clues about their sexual orientations or how they will see themselves, but knowing that they will be loved no matter who they are is the foundation their future lives depend upon. A 2019 study by the Trevor Report showed that LGBTQ young adults who have at least one supportive adult in their lives are forty percent less likely to become suicidal. I know they have other influences and will be bombarded by media and peer influence as they venture out into the world. Yet I have the chance to provide a foundation for how my children filter all that they will encounter out there. Why would I not put myself to the trouble of explaining my own ongoing efforts to understand and empathize with other people? Congregations are among the few places where people who hold different views can still grapple together with what our values say about how we treat one another. If we do not have these conversations at church, where else will we do so?

When the parable of the prodigal son was read in church recently, I could not help wondering why we are so impressed by the father's welcome back of his wayward son. Of course, he ran to him with open arms when the son was still far off. Is this supposed to be remarkable? Is it not what every parent would do? Or maybe it is noticeable for a father figure because we have so overly burdened that role with traits like judgment and tough love. If it were a mother in the story, would this be an obvious response? Made from our own DNA or not, raising our children is such a part of our own identities that without them a part of us is lost. Upon a prodigal child's return, that part of us is found again. What a relief. What a gift, to be able to try again. Even if the road to reconciliation is miles long, at least we can be ourselves with them present, while we travel it together.

Conventional wisdom invites us to count silently to ten before responding in emotionally fraught scenarios. We can restate what we think we heard or observed. We might make soothing physical contact like a hug or holding a hand before responding to calm us both down. On my best days, I parent like this. Sometimes as a pastor, I become very aware of forcing my facial muscles into a neutral look, especially my eyebrows. I know I have to model empathy if I want anyone looking to me for guidance to learn it. It can feel like an out-of-body experience to suppress our first responses. So the best I can do is regulate my own expressions, ask for forgiveness when I fail, and try again.

The church has been complicit in discrimination and weak theology that does not stand with oppressed people. We have major work of repentance and reparation ahead of us. I want people to stay around long enough to be transformed by this hard work of self-awareness and listening to others' trauma, some of which the church has inflicted. If I lose them by appearing "too political," I miss the opportunity to have even these fraught conversations. Jesus was very clear about us taking care of the poor and vulnerable ones. That is not up for debate, yet nearly every group of vulnerable people in need of support from the church has been turned into a political target for hatred. The mothering finesse of assuring "our" people that they are loved, while calling them to account, requires much practice. Sometimes we get it wrong. Sometimes we reach out beautifully. All the time it is stressful.

When we parents were coached in ECFE (early childhood family education) to give our children a choice as a way to move things forward, I was amazed at how well our older daughter responded. When she would be fooling around instead of getting her shoes on to go somewhere, I could say, "Are you going to put your shoes on yourself, or should I put them on your feet?" Almost always, when given the chance to do something herself rather than have it done for/to her, she chose to do it herself. Of course, either option had to be a real possibility that I would accept as an outcome. I wonder if this would work with congregations? What might have happened had I explicitly given the congregation the choice after that major church-wide vote, and said, "Are you going to examine your theology and see if God's love includes LGBTQ people, or are you going to trust that others have done faithful discernment and go with their decision?" Either way, I should have held myself and the congregation to options that engaged instead of buried the issue.

During our "joys and concerns" time on the Sunday after the 2009 church-wide vote, one Liberian patriarch said, "We heard your sermon, Pastor. But what do *you* think about gay people?" I knew that my stance would be taken as God's or they would leave the church over it. "I think you loved each other as brothers and sisters last week, and you still belong to each other this week, too," I replied. I should not have said something so practical. I should have said something theological instead. I was managing my own anxiety about conflict instead of moving the conversation forward, or at least bringing it out in the open. Did this incident start or perpetuate a pattern of me hiding my own beliefs? What we ignore or look past in order to function as a "family" or congregational unit is not as relevant in the end as how God relates to us. I regret not preaching about God's boundless love for her LGBTQ children, regardless of the cost to my leadership.

Most important is what God the Parent does. God tries again and again to relate to us in different ways. God adapts and tries different approaches to reach more of those whom Abraham's offspring are to bless. The incarnation of Jesus builds the relationship between us and God. Jesus embodies mothering with his own human responses and physical sacrifices. After Jesus's resurrection, the Holy Spirit takes this embodiment into the world, to reside in each of us who are seeking to do God's will. She hides within our neighbors and neighborhoods, surprising and challenging us. Consider the depth of vulnerability to which God opens herself, by parenting in different ways to assure all of us we are beloved.

The most powerful tool in our clergy mother toolbox is theology: we belong to each other because we belong to God who loves us all. God continually adapts in love, so that we can stay in relationship and show the world the love we experience from God.

It Gets Personal

Is there any other job in which one's marriage and family are considered part of the package, in the way a pastor's is? Congregations sometimes describe themselves as "a family," but clergy are a strange part of that unit. A clergy person who is also a mother, with all the cultural assumptions about domestic responsibilities and blame or credit that belong to mothers, inhabits an even stranger space. How much transference can we hold: from members' emotional responses to God, to their mothers, to their family dynamics? Congregation members may imagine or feel a closeness to the pastor, yet there is also a real distance between the parts of our lives we share with members and those we do not. Our interpersonal skills are paramount to job performance. Yet somehow our familial relationships are mixed up in there too, including our marital status or struggles, our spouse's involvement or lack thereof in the life of the church, and our children's behavior inside and outside of the church. There is a weight to the collective gaze of a congregation upon us and our family. What is the toll of the emotional labor we do to hide when we are hurt, angered, or worn out by members of the "church family"?

"Pastor, we need to talk." From a parenting standpoint, apologizing and calling others out on their need to seek forgiveness is foundational to our role. Apologizing makes me more accessible to my kids or to parishioners. But this short sentence still sends shivers down my spine: "We need to talk." The pastor's child's behavior is bound to be a topic of conversation among church leadership at some point, perhaps many. Maybe my little darling is the one biting others in the church's preschool, the one who is too loud or active or not "properly behaved" during worship. Maybe my preteen is testing limits in confirmation, or my teenager is talking trash about youth group. Perhaps my young adult child no longer participates in church. When the pastor gets pulled aside to talk about her family, it is hard not to feel defensive, in both directions. We probably already have feelings about our kids' behavior, but now we have feelings about our congregants' handling of it, too. Clergy mothers are always an uncomfortable case study with which to talk about our church's culture. What happens if we express it when we think we are owed an apology, or if we apologize for our own mistakes? Can we craft solutions between clergy and laity that do not put all the weight on one of us, but unfold it so that many people can hold onto a corner? As much as I do not want my family to be in the spotlight, if it is anyway, we can at least have frank conversation about expectations, using my family as the example.

Do you have in-laws? Extended family? Neighbors? Negotiating those relationships for the well-being of our kids while hoping for healthy influences and a sense of community may feel similar to coaching a congregation into positive relationships with their surrounding neighborhood. A pastor cannot help a bias toward her congregation, a defensiveness, even. We want others to love them, or at least to think well of them. We also feel the pull of caring for those Jesus called "the least of these, my children," who may or may not be inside the church. How we approach the opening of hearts and minds to new family members matters deeply. Before adopting our older daughter, my husband and I were part of an "adoption book club," a group of friends who were all in the adoption process. We all were developing language to talk to our parents, siblings, and others about how our children through adoption would be "ours" and "real" and belong completely and forever in our family. We intended to model, provide reading materials, and address directly the language and interactions we wanted our children to have with our extended families. The way we lead this conversation and frame it is key.

Some of the prospective parents in our adoption book club were anticipating transracial adoptions, so considering how their extended families talk about and interact with people of different races was already something they discussed, set expectations around, and worried about. Their relationships with parents and family were about to change, or at least be greatly affected by how the extended family received their children. Many Lutheran churches in Minnesota still strongly identify with the ethnic heritage of their founding members. When I am coaching a congregation to create space for new family members, it is more than fair for a loving clergy mother to ask, "How does celebrating your ethnic background help or hinder identifying with the folks now living around the church? Why is a congregation so white in a neighborhood that has not been majority white in decades?" I know we feel defensive about this, as if pride in our ancestry is something we have been doing wrong. Maybe it is—racism or white supremacy should have no place in Christianity. Maybe the long-standing lutefisk dinner and other marks of Scandinavian heritage are just less relevant to who we want to become than who we were in the past. It is not how we need to move forward for the sake of relating to the newest members of our family. As a mother protecting her children and a pastor leading a congregation, I know my focus must be on the most vulnerable. It is up to those of us who never doubted that we belonged to create that sense for our new members. For those who have never felt welcome in a homogenous white church touting its (for example) Scandinavian ancestry, the insiders need to do the work of acting like family with the newest members until it becomes true.

Mothers and pastors are changed while trying to love our families into developing empathy. Our own weaknesses are exposed. Perhaps the least trustworthy pastor is one who stays on the pedestal, unaffected. When the pastor's family seems perfect, it is perfectly suspect. Congregations who hold their pastor as better than everyone else may represent God as inaccessible and unaffected by us, too. We can trust a pastor (and a God) whose very investment in us makes them vulnerable to being impacted by our lives. As Jesus says in Matthew 5:11, "Blessed are you when people revile you and persecute you and utter all kinds of evil against you falsely on my account." We are blessed when the ire of others is aimed toward us on account of the children we love.

QUESTIONS FOR REFLECTION

Clergy Mothers:

1. What emotions do you most struggle with showing in your public role as pastor?

2. What effects do you feel on your person, for the labor of disguising your emotions, tempering your responses and serving people who anger or hurt you?

3. When has the emotional labor of being a mother informed your ministry, and vice versa?

Support Network:

1. When have you been most aware of the emotional labor you perform at home, work or other contexts?

2. How does naming the different allegiances and requirements of empathy for a clergy mother affect your understanding of their role?

CHAPTER 8

Who Is the Church for Us?

When asked how my husband and I met, I have to admit, "in church." I am very quick to add, ". . . but I was not his pastor!" If it is not immediately apparent, that would have crossed some crucial boundaries, not to mention made life exponentially more complicated. To be someone's pastor implies a power dynamic, both spiritually and socially. A pastor is also a public figure, in whose life many in a congregation or community are interested. "Dating the pastor" courts attention and scrutiny that a new relationship does not need. What if you break up with a church member? What if it is traumatic?

Beginning with the story of dating my eventual husband is a clear way to illustrate you cannot "pastor" your own family. This is also a very good reason why my parents, if they lived in our city, should not become members of a church where I am the pastor (oh, but imagine the extra childcare during worship). I cannot be a pastor to my mother or father, because I cannot leave my role as their adult daughter in order to do so. Our family system would bleed into the church's family system. This same dynamic is why pastors cannot fully be reciprocal "friends" with congregants. The roles can obscure one another or hurt others who do not experience this closeness with the pastor. Eventually we might have to have a painful breakup or step back from the relationship, and everyone is hurt.

Bringing Our Family to Church

Pastors all make choices about how to integrate our families into church life, or whether to look outside of the congregation for faith community. Every clergy parent has to do what works for their family, and we need to trust them to understand that best choice better than anyone else. However, if the choices are made because of a lack of support, a congregation could make more options possible. For single clergy mothers or clergy couples, childcare adds a layer of anxiety to our biggest day of ministry leadership. If the parents are a clergy couple with two churches, the choice may be about whose congregation the children go to, not only for Sundays, but all their engagement in church. Some clergy actually need to choose to have the children at home with a babysitter on Sunday mornings because of specific behavioral needs or choices surrounding each spouse's attention on their work. Obviously, our faith is important to us and we want our children to be nurtured in the faith by a community, too. But when do the benefits outweigh the stress?

A pastor's choices may be a reality check for the congregation about our support for parents in general: What does our church do with the youngest children? How does our congregation support parents in bringing their older children to worship? When parents' management of their children in church becomes a greater burden than the perceived value of belonging, for a pastor's kid or any children, it is a problem for all of us. The pastor's family's choices also reveal that Sunday is a very long day for most pastors. Beyond worship and education time, it is also often the time members wish to meet with the pastor, committees may try to meet, and confirmation programming or other events are scheduled (because we are more likely to get people to participate if they are already there). Yet there may be paid childcare in the nursery only during worship, if then. Throw in the need for lunch and naps for our youngest family members and subjecting them to Mom's schedule is not quality parenting.

So how do clergy mothers include our children in the congregation's ministries, without adding more to our own obligations in leading a congregation? Strategies my colleagues have shared include hiring a babysitter to bring the children to church, sit with them in worship, take them to and from children's programming, and take them home afterward. Others have "church grandmas" who do the same, although using volunteers within the congregation can have its own complications. Some of us have spouses or partners available and willing to engage in the life of the congregation with our children and for their own sake. This was certainly the expectation when all clergy spouses were wives, and their uncompensated role was its own job. How are expectations different for a pastor's husband? Some clergy spouses claim different religious traditions, are agnostic, or simply are not engaged spiritually by the offerings at our particular congregation. Any way this goes, clergy mothers are hyperaware of how our children's perceptions and attitudes toward church are being shaped by others, not ourselves.

In addition to negotiating how our spouse and children will be present at church, clergy mothers may also agonize over our own level of energy or effort in supporting their faith at home, like every other parent. Do they like reading their Bible? Do we have rituals? Do we pray as a family more than haphazardly? My relationship to my work can seep into what I have the energy to do at home. Maybe admitting that dynamic is motivation to lean on their godparents more for our children's spiritual development. How do we help our older children process the burden of knowing everyone is watching them at church as the pastor's kid or the weirdness of people acting like they know you, although you do not recognize them? Can we help them separate the experience of congregational life as the pastor's kid and their Christian faith? Our vulnerability about this perceived failing may not be something we are willing to claim in public, but with certain parenting peers, it would be a dose of authenticity to admit when we are floundering or looking for suggestions.

Occasionally all other options fall through and the plan is actually for our child to be up front with us while we lead. It is certainly not a foolproof plan, but sometimes it works, because it has to. Our child sits in the pulpit at our feet while we preach, or behind the altar as we preside. A video of a male college professor holding a student's baby so he can participate in class went viral. My mother raves about how adorable it is when their male senior pastor carries babies around the sanctuary after a baptism; one time he decided it was so fun he held the infant through his entire sermon. A photo of a woman giving her election night acceptance speech with her daughter at her feet behind the podium was rapidly shared in all my clergy women networks. I imagine other moms might experience this feeling of solidarity when they see a clergy mom, parenting and leading simultaneously. Given the limited availability of earned sick and safe time in multiple fields, what mom has not had to take her child with her to work at least once?

My hunch is that this visual is most heartwarming when mothering in our professional spheres is the exception, and not the pattern. As worshipers see clergy women more and more in the role of mother, hidden prejudices may surface in attitudes about women or younger people in leadership. Staff and parishioners may forget to speak to her as pastor and begin commenting as they would to a daughter or granddaughter. We know it happens, so we try to guard against it. I wonder how much of this is because our most deeply embedded associations with "Pastor" are still male? Because "Pastor" was a male term for so long, God seemed to be too, leaning into the fatherly disciplinary metaphor more and more. Who speaks about that discrimination in our midst? Is it just the clergy mothers who vent to each other in a closed Facebook group, or could someone in the congregation proactively say things out loud at regular intervals, such as:

> Pastor's mothering of her child while preaching the gospel shows me how God does both: cares for our emotional needs and challenges us.

Or:

> Mother Jane doesn't stop being a mom to be a pastor. Each of us have multiple callings, and God uses the mixture within us to make our unique witness.

Or even:

> I'm starting to see how Christian ministry is also like parenting—especially for mothers—and seeing Reverend Sue with her family and with us makes me think about how God guides all of us as children of God.

It is complicated for clergy mothers to do this advocacy for ourselves because it seems self-serving. We point out, however, that the first ones to discover the possibility of resurrection on Easter were the women, because they went to care for the body. Some of them were mothers; all of them culturally caregivers, who were then given the task of spreading the Word. Christians should not be able to share anything about the resurrection of Jesus without embracing the caregiving and humility of the mothering role. The mothers whose hearts are broken beyond repair by the loss of Jesus (including Jesus's mother, Mary) are the most reliable guarantee that the gospel will continue to spread. God will keep going like a mother, through mothers, even after the unthinkable has happened.

When God's relationship with humanity is broken, she feels it, and cries out for response. The Old Testament prophets lament with God's brokenheartedness spilling out in their words. "Return, O faithless children," says the Lord in Jeremiah 3, "I thought how I would set you among my children, and give you a pleasant land, the most beautiful heritage of all the nations. And I thought you would call me, My Father, and would not turn from following me. Return, O faithless children, I will heal your faithlessness." I recognize that wistfulness, disappointment, and desperate appeal for a change of behavior. I, too, thought parenting would be different; I thought that if I loved my children well enough, they would reciprocate with obedience. Sometimes they do, but often they do not. God's mothering love also comes across through the prophet Malachi: "They shall be mine, says the Lord of hosts, my special possession on the day when I act, and I will spare them as parents spare their children who serve them" (3:17). That is exactly the determination we need to persevere in parenthood.

Jesus did not live on God's love alone; even as an adult teacher and healer, others provided food, arranged where he would stay, and sometimes intercepted those who wanted to see him. Of course, culturally, the women who traveled with them would have done much of this caregiving, unnoticed and unrecorded in scripture. Practically, but symbolically, women drew the water needed for everyone to live. The male disciples took care of Jesus, too. The incident when Jesus rebuked the disciples for trying to direct children away from him saying, "let the little children come to me" (Matt. 19:14), was probably not the only time they ran interference. Jesus's disciples were his hands and feet, distributing loaves and fishes to thousands, and setting out on the Sea of Galilee so Jesus could get a little time away. He took them with him to the Garden of Gethsemane and asked them to keep watch and pray with him. Even after his death, the women were there to tend to his body. Nobody could replace Jesus's role in their relationships, but he modeled receiving care, too, from his flawed but loving "family members."

Unlike with our earthly parents, there will never come a time when our roles are reversed and God will be dependent on us for caregiving. Our relationship with our heavenly Mother cannot ever dissipate with our maturity. She never ceases to care for us, anticipate our needs, binding her emotions up in our well-being. There is a mutuality that is fundamental to this relationship between God and us. It upsets the religious authorities when Jesus refers to God as Father, because children have influence upon their parents, so it is a bit like equating himself with God. The closeness we have with God as God's children is undeniable but the trajectory of this parent-child relationship is different from our earthly pattern. God will still mother me, still pastor me, regardless of the responsibilities of maturity I assume or lay down.

Would we say that the Holy Spirit needs or is encouraged by reciprocity from us? When I teach or preach about the Holy Spirit, I find myself using phrases like "creating space for the Holy Spirit to work," "openness to the movement of the Spirit" or "listening to what the Holy Spirit might be saying to us." No one can guide, nurture, or reinforce love for us without us allowing them the space to do so. So while I do not know how to identify the emotional response or attachment coming from the Spirit, perhaps we can say that she needs our responses in order to accomplish her caregiving work. She also seems to make it possible for us to be open to her actions. When this Advocate intercedes for us, "with sighs too deep for words to express" (Rom. 8:26), the solidarity we experience primes our responses for the future. I still tell the experience of peace I felt after praying during the third grade, anxious because my family had to move to another state for my father's new job. That experience formed me into who I am and is the reason I consider "faith" to be my most prominent spiritual gift. The Holy Spirit works through the church universal and in specific congregations, though obviously that plan is not sin-proof. Still, the space between us can be holy, as the Holy Spirit works on all of our hearts, moving us to better love each other and creation.

Who Pastors or Mothers Us?

A friend reminded me recently that our children reflect our state of mind and behaviors to such a degree that they begin to care for us long before they step into the role of caregivers. Relationships are mutual, even when lopsided. Children minister to our needs for tender touch, words of encouragement, and of course reminders of why we work so hard. I recorded the exact day our second child smiled deliberately as a newborn—November 19—because that reciprocity could keep me going for hours. A snuggle, seeing them playing a pastor or mom during imaginative play, or a veiled compliment from a teenager reminds us we do not have to forge ahead alone. At church, when a child draws a picture of me in the act of leading worship, or a confirmation parent reports their child quoting me, it reinforces my sense of calling.

Multiple colleagues keep a file of thank you notes in our desks to raise our spirits when we are frustrated, remembering the better times. One member of the committee that hired me at my very first church—where we also got married—sends my husband and me an anniversary card every year, now twelve years later and living in a different state. To be remembered is so touching. A weekend at a member's cabin (without them present) has been such a gift of love to us. The gift of time away together is so precious, it almost cannot be measured. Scripture tells of Lydia, a dealer in purple cloth, who prevailed upon the apostles in the book of Acts to stay in her home, to share her resources (Acts 16:14–15). Women of prominence Joanna and Susanna also provided for Jesus and the disciples out of their resources (Luke 8:3). For these supportive church mothers, we give thanks.

Beyond unexpected gifts or hospitality, a pastor's salary comes from the offering plate. The church provides for us as the women provided for Jesus (although we are clearly not Jesus). At the end of his life, there is that detail: "Many women were also there, looking on from a distance; they had followed Jesus from Galilee and had provided for him. Among them were Mary Magdalene, and Mary the mother of James and Joseph, and the mother of the sons of Zebedee" (Matt. 27:55–56). As priests and pastors, our livelihood is supported by our congregation's giving. When my first congregation increased my associate pastor salary because it had been under the synod guidelines, I knew it was a stretch for them. Yet it made a big difference for me as a single person just starting out, as well as valuing in the budget the work I did. My family currently gives to the church where we are members, not only out of gratitude for their care for us, but specifically to support a woman pastor in leadership. For clergy who are partnered and have a spouse who is employed, that second income can relieve the financial burden working for the church can bring with it, but that should not be expected by a congregation. I have the freedom to do less-than-full-time interim work because my spouse has a full-time job with medical benefits, but I know that is a privilege other clergy do not have.

The flexibility of this sort of ministry can be a burden or a gift or fluctuates between the two. To be able to volunteer at my kids' school during the day, or work on a sermon from home when one of my children is sick is invaluable. Yet this flexibility means pastors may feel obligated to say "yes" to meetings or Saturday events more often to signify that we are putting in our time.

I cannot always compartmentalize my thoughts about my family or congregation, but sometimes a change of scenery or physical activity helps me to process in ways I otherwise would not. Walking meetings are the best. I invited church council members to walk the neighborhood with me during the day at my first church. It got us moving, while also noticing our community and talking to each other. Years later, walking the blocks around our home with the stroller gave the kids and me a chance to breathe, notice things together, and talk. Now that my kids are a bit older, I make it to a yoga class twice a week like it is my job, because clearing my head while stretching my muscles is such a help to my attitude and body. Honestly though, my favorite thing is when the instructor says, "Beautiful!" to our poses, and gently talks us through meditation. Her voice takes care of me, gives me space to bid farewell to all the other thoughts, and just be. I am myself then. It is part of our work to be healthy. Church meetings need to be scheduled when people are available, which happens to be in the evening, when our children are home from school too. That might mean we have to carve out exercise or wellness time for ourselves during the day.

The reciprocity of breastfeeding is one way to describe what it is like to be sustained by the very same exhausting service that also drains our energy. Breastfeeding is not always possible, for a whole host of reasons, biological or societal. It worked for us, but wow, was it intense! I marveled that my body produced food for another human being, and our daughter grew and was healthy. Her nursing not only boosted my milk supply, but also stimulated the hormones that sustained my motherly attachment and caregiving, as sleep deprived as I was. The very action that woke me multiple times a night, gave me secret twinges and occasionally intense pain, and solidified my commitment to the relationship. This is not everyone's experience, but I sometimes thought I was parenting on oxytocin alone.

Julian of Norwich, a medieval mystic, describes Jesus Christ feeding us from his own body, an unabashed reference to breastfeeding. The image shows up in medieval artwork. Remarkably, Jesus seems not to resent the destruction we cause his physical body. Instead, breaking his body and spilling his blood to feed us strengthened his love and attachment to us. With his last breath, Jesus begged God to forgive us, because we know not what we do. On the cross, a Roman soldier pierced his side and both blood and water poured out. Jesus feeds us still through the sacraments, from his own body. Astonishingly it increases his love, when he sustains us through his broken body, joining us to his Body.

Whether they are every-Sunday attendees or not, our families will likely mark their milestones within our congregations. The congregation may be delighted by this, but we will wonder: how can I be the mom and the pastor at the same time? About two months after our older daughter joined our family through adoption, we had her baptized in the congregation where I was the only pastor. I needed to be "Mama" first and foremost. For one, I was probably the only person she would have tolerated lifting her two-and-a-half-year-old body up to reach the font. Having had exclusively female caregivers in her home country before we adopted her, she gradually warmed to my husband, but her responses were unpredictable. There are no other clergy in my family tree. While the bishop is described as "the pastor to the pastors" in my Lutheran denomination, a friend and colleague from a nearby church, also an adoptive mama, was our "conference dean" at the time, a set of responsibilities that meant she convened the area pastors for meetings. I quoted that authoritative title when I explained why we had invited her to baptize our daughter, but if I am honest, it was because as an adoptive mother, I knew she would speak with sensitivity about our particular family situation. Baptism carries a lot of "welcome to the family" imagery, and to be able to trust this pastor with that was important for me.

Other clergy mother colleagues have shared how they navigated their children's milestones in the congregation, especially confirmation and weddings. Clergy mothers also want to be the proud parent, the tears-streaming-down-her-face parent if that is how we roll, and to let the event be about our child's participation in the faith community, not ours. Is it fair to say that the main source of stress as these significant events approach is anticipating a congregation's perception that our mothering role might be overshadowing our pastoral role? One of the congregations I served had a story about the color of the carpet in the sanctuary being changed in the same year the organist's daughter was married there. The colors of the bridal party went so well with the carpet that rumors flew: "Don't you know her mom was on the committee that chose that color, and I bet it was because of the wedding!" Imagine if the bride's mother had been the pastor.

Long before I was a mother, I became engaged and was married in the first congregation I served as pastor. The joy of that occasion was not overtaken by hassle primarily because of one woman, a pastor's widow whose own daughters had been married in congregations her husband had led. That dear lady consulted us on foods, then created a directed potluck to feed our friends and the congregation following the wedding service. She was aware of congregation and clergy dynamics: how people lovingly want to help but that too many voices could become a problem. She was a godsend to us.

We completed our premarital counseling through a private counselor. Clearly, any counseling that a pastor's children or spouses might seek from a pastor needs to be directed elsewhere, from premarital counseling to therapeutic or spiritual angst. We talk about these worries as any family members might do, but not in a pastoral role. Most people within a congregation may not realize how significant a clergy person's role is as the first resource in times of grief or mental health crises. Our families will need to turn to a person outside of the congregation, and perhaps even outside of our denominational and regional colleagues, as their designated counseling resource. Who fulfills the role of pastor in our lives during ordinary time? Motherhood and pastorhood are both endurance races, building up trust with the "ministry of presence" over time. "Who pastors the pastor?" resonates in the same way the question asked in the mommy-blogging world does: "Who mothers the mother?" Who is our reliable caregiving presence in the background until we need them to step into the foreground? With whom can we, our spouses, or our children wrestle with our own faith questions, without it becoming a threat to our family source of income (the pastor's job)? With whom can we process what church dynamics are doing to our relationships with God or each other? Just as our families need a pastoral or therapeutic option outside our parish or denomination, so, too, do clergy need a spiritual director or trusted friend with whom they can wrestle with faith questions, process work-related stresses and joys, and pray.

This potential vacancy in our own spiritual support system is one reason it behooves clergy mothers to develop our understanding of God as Mother. A heavenly Mother could carry the weight of these relationships along with us. She will mother us and pastor us, with equal parts empathy and "kick-in-the-pants." The Holy Spirit is my favorite illustration of the ever-present advocate God promises to be for us, who will do even greater things than Jesus, scripture assures us. The Spirit supports us so that we can multiply the work of God in the world. Yet how do we best perceive the presence of the Holy Spirit? My own spiritual practices can be intertwined with the work of ministry. As I pray through my prayer list, I am constantly drawn back into the "faith community" that may also be exhausting me. When I worship, I am also working. When I read scripture—even as a devotional practice—I always have an ear tuned to "that'll preach." I need some creative spiritual outlets to get me out of work mode so that I may simply enjoy the presence of God, tenderly caring for me. For this reason, I love singing in worship at gatherings of pastors. It is an unselfconscious delight. I have tried individual and group spiritual direction but felt like I am not very good at it. I get impatient with pondering the directions the Spirit is moving me separate from the plans I want to make, but I suppose God knows that about me already. Supportive colleague groups, especially of women, have been spiritually uplifting for me. Unsurprisingly, I hear the Spirit most clearly through other clergy mothers, who through the solidarity of our joys and struggles, are able to encourage and challenge each other.

Clergy mothers need our colleagues, but we also need our therapists. Our theology and relational ministry bumps up against the stress of leading, perceived constant observation, and emotional labor. We need, at the very least, to find counselors or therapists with a grasp not only of spiritual matters, but of the paradox of theology and complicated enmeshment that can be a faith community. When one's family is so affected by the "family" of a church, we need someone who understands it enough to help us recognize unhealthy patterns.

Who will embody this Spirit, these mothering behaviors of God, for my spouse? My husband asked early on—noticing how much I appreciated Young Clergy Women International—if there is a "pastor's husbands" online group. There is something about just hanging around with others who "get it," listening in, sharing the small stuff or big, until one day it is my crisis that needs some help. Being mothered is resting in the presence we can count on when we need it, but (in the best way possible) take for granted when we do not. Adults all need peers, so we can mutually mother each other. We can reinforce for each other that our mothering God loves us, enough to respect our independence, but cheer us on.

QUESTIONS FOR REFLECTION

Clergy Women:

1. Who have been your key spiritual support people, or spiritual practices for "filling your cup"?
2. When has a congregation taken good care of you or your family?
3. What are some of your family's faith resources outside the congregation?
4. When has your role as pastor created a joyful memory for you or your family?

Support Network:

1. What "feeds" you spiritually, and how/when do you tend to that need?
2. How do you share or spread out the responsibility for tending your children's faith?
3. Which of the struggles or joys described in clergy women's lives in this chapter resonated with an experience from your own life?

CHAPTER 9

∾

Mother to One,
Mother to All

In the beginning, the only word we heard her say was the one that means "no." Our older daughter was two-and-a-half years old when she joined our family, but spoke hardly five words in her first language. She did not have the repeated stimulation of a caregiver connecting face-to-face regularly during those first months of her life, the way in which most of us learn how to speak. She certainly could communicate without words, but I also adapted to reading her body language, maintaining solid routines, offering her options, and anticipating her needs. Inside our relationship it worked. To go outside of our family and have her voice heard, though, our daughter would have to learn to speak up. Advocacy begins at home.

I am convinced that the skills and passions honed by raising children are not meant to stay within our narrow definitions of family. There are two directions our fierce advocacy for our children might turn, however, depending on the story we are hearing about what being a mother means. First, there is the story of scarcity: that there are not enough resources for our children and others, so we must grasp and keep whatever we can in order for our children to thrive. Sometimes we share our hoarded resources with those who are close to us, but never those who might call into question our layers of privilege. Second, there is the story of abundance: there are more than enough resources for all, and in fact we are nourished and equipped for the purpose of sharing the abundance with others. All children belong to us because they, too, are children of God. The two stories point a mother's gaze in opposite directions, inward or outward.

Congregations still have significant power to shape which story our communities believe and act upon. Media and entertainment outlets get consumers' attention by deploying the story of scarcity, so we will buy or consume or click on their spin to somehow mask our fear. Pastors and preachers may neglect calling out those scare tactics for fear it will be seen as "too political" or hinder our relationships with parishioners. Other preachers seem to promote an "us-versus-them" scarcity mentality. In my current interim position, I am preaching the news alongside the gospel. To some degree, the freedom of being temporary gives me special license to push the controversial buttons. However, my experience as a mother also compels me to speak up for those whose voices this congregation might not otherwise hear. I do not explicitly teach or preach about mothering often, but it is the strength behind my resolve when I preach against injustice or respond with compassion to God's children ravaged by disasters. God loves us all with the ferocity of a mother. We are called to care for all God's children.

God wants abundance for us. Jesus describes abundant care and trust in the midst of threats with a parable about a thief and a shepherd in John 10. He emphasizes how crucial the shepherd's voice is in leading the sheep where they need to go. They follow as the shepherd repeats their names, trusting the voice of their caregiver. "The thief comes only to steal and kill and destroy. I came that they may have life, and have it abundantly" (John 10:10). Is it the promise of abundance they follow? Perhaps we are not as thoughtful as that. For sheep, and perhaps for all who rely on a caregiver, it is more about the voice, the feeling and experience of trust for the one who has taken care of us thus far. We follow to abundant life when we have been well loved.

Navigating Jealousy

Jealousy may be the first barrier to moving people from a mentality of scarcity to one of abundance. God deals with human jealousy regularly, beginning with the sibling rivalry of Cain and Abel. When each of these brothers gave offerings to God,

> the Lord had regard for Abel and his offering, but for Cain and his offering he had no regard. So Cain was very angry and his countenance fell. The Lord said to Cain, "Why are you angry and why has your countenance fallen? If you do well, will you not be accepted? And if you do not do well, sin is lurking at the door; its desire is for you but you must master it."
>
> Genesis 4:4b–7

Cain kills his brother Abel out of jealousy, and utters the infamous line, "Am I my brother's keeper?" in response to God's confrontation about his whereabouts. Of course he is. God curses Cain's ability to reap food from the earth and declares that he will be a wanderer. God metes out justice, for no matter our history or circumstances, we are responsible for our actions. Then God offers hope and a sign of Cain's belonging to God, so that others would not do to him what he has done out of jealousy to his brother.

Perhaps this is the opening to guide people away from jealous responses and into advocacy. "Am I my brother's keeper?" The answer is yes, we are. It is nothing other than sin to let our jealousy, justified or not, take lives. If we are jealous our paychecks did not increase it does not justify cruelty to migrants from Latin America. No feelings of jealousy or fear or scarcity justify abandoning our siblings to death. Now how to express this in ways people can hear: God loves you, and yes, God expects you to speak up for your sibling, not claim what is happening to them is none of your business.

We do not have to love God's actions that set the Cain and Abel plot line in motion, nor defend them. God has no regard for Cain's offering, and instead of lashing out at God, Cain turns his anger on his brother. When we yearn to be loved or accepted, we can do horrible things. Yet is it God's fault that we are feeling jealous? How do we handle our perceptions of how God feels about us? Could we not check out those feelings with God, or someone else who knows God well? Is murdering the other we jealously think has gotten the attention our only option?

Our congregations are full of people who are hurt by how they think God has treated them. Maybe there are circumstances in their lives that they believe God should have protected them from, or people who are telling them that God does not accept the things they do, or who they are. God is fiercely jealous as well, but mostly about us not having any other gods. God still loves leaders like King David (although he took Bathsheba and had her husband killed) and the apostle Paul (who persecuted all the Christians he could find before his conversion), which tells us that God's jealousy is paired with fierce mercy, when we keep returning to God.

Defining Terms and Sorting through Memories

A major step in coaching people to speak up for themselves and each other is making meaning of the words we use and hear. My children mostly ask these tough questions while I am driving, for some reason. Why did Jesus die on a cross? What is "divorced"? What are "weapons"? The questions are different at church, and more often I am the one asking them. What does it mean to be an "ally"? What is the Second Amendment about? Why don't we say "illegals" in talking about people?

When the worst words come out of the mouths of those we love, there may not be much time to summarize the hurt they represent, so we need a two-part strategy. First, we can prepare by having preemptive conversations when the stakes seem lower—when we are not in public with others listening in, or reacting to an incendiary current event. Second, we practice concise, respectful responses that can refer to further conversation.

Jennifer Harvey talks about different stages for opening and deepening conversations about race with children in her 2017 book *Raising White Kids: Bringing Up Children in a Racially Unjust America.* The end goal is not simply raising children who are not overtly racist. This is not enough. Instead, we want to prepare our children to become anti-racist, standing and speaking against injustice. Parents can begin by honoring children's natural tendency to notice differences, rather than being embarrassed about it. If we communicate that there is something wrong with noticing difference—"we are colorblind"—then our children will never learn to recognize and combat discrimination. They will not have the vocabulary or practice to talk about injustice. Neither will they trust the adults who have brushed off their questions. This applies to congregational life. "We are all God's children" should not be a way to dismiss the differences in how people are treated or to avoid talking about systemic injustice.

In the congregation, clergy mothers know we have much to discuss. We need to debrief the encounters that have made an impression on us. We need to process the news, as uncomfortable as that makes us. How do we check in about what has happened since last we were together? My family shares "highs and lows" around the dinner table; the church we belong to also calls a time in our worship service "milestones," which the pastor describes as "the highs and lows of our week." If we do not check in, how will we know what is going on in each other's lives, other than gossip? How will we shape our interpretations of events through the lens of faith? Pastors have multiple opportunities to lead an examination of what is happening around us, including from the pulpit. The sermon is a time to interpret how God is speaking through scripture and our current experiences, bringing to our attention voices we might not consider otherwise. What does our faith say about the way we are living on this earth together?

In her book *Wearing God*, Lauren Winner admits that exploring images of God has revealed much about her own biases. She had been picturing God as a middle-class white mother laboring and giving birth. When she learned from women she taught in the prison system what it is like to give birth while wearing shackles and anticipating having the newborn taken away, the image intensified considerably. Similarly, consider the income lost by a middle-class mother who chooses to stay home and breastfeed a child for half a year. It is a sacrifice for mothers with partners, but more so for a single mother doing shift work with no place designated to pump. God sees the metaphors we are capable of grasping and takes them into "more so" territory as well. The prophet Isaiah asks on God's behalf, "Can a woman forget her nursing child, or show no compassion for the child of her womb? Even these may forget, yet I will not forget you" (49:10). Jesus's sayings include this one: "Is there anyone among you who, if your child asks for bread, will give a stone? Or if the child asks for a fish, will give a snake? If you then, who are evil, know how to give good gifts to your children, how much more will your Father in heaven give good things to those who ask him!" (Matt. 7: 9–11). Our experience is only the beginning of understanding the extent of God's loving parenting. It is also only the beginning of human experience, broadening our view outward to those parents doing this hard work in contexts different from our own. My story is not the only one, by a long shot. Scripture expands the parenting analogies upward and outward from our own limited experiences.

Sorting through the baggage we have from our parents is as essential to becoming independent adults as learning to cook and do our own laundry. If we can actually recognize what we got from older generations—before we turn into them—then we can choose what we want to keep or leave behind. Otherwise, when under stress (a given of parenting) we revert to the patterns with which we were raised. When we have an understanding of family systems, clergy mothers can be particularly adept at leading the "church family" to name and choose our patterns of behavior, instead of becoming unconsciously overtaken by them.

As institutional churches decline and wane in influence, American Christians need to sort through how we will define ourselves. It may feel like God has no regard for what we are offering, because many of our congregations are not prospering. When our congregations celebrate an anniversary and we share old photographs of a full sanctuary, we need help processing the responses that rise within us. We also need to be honest about the oppression of women and minorities during the "good old days," and how our congregation has responded to waves of immigrants after the ones that formed us. Major anniversaries require careful telling of the story so that we can repent past actions, while choosing who we will be going forward. This may not be the joyful reminiscing we want to participate in, but it must be done. It is the pastor's task to empathize with those who feel the loss of the past, even when we do not see it that way, while not leaving the family stuck in nostalgia. Learning new ways to share the gospel in our time strikes me as more faithful than perpetuating old patterns.

Many of our churches are or will be at a major decision point in the next decade. Will we choose to use our remaining resources of faithful people, property, or money on ourselves until they dwindle down to nothing? Or, will we step out in faith to generously declare God's love for our neighbors? Will we give ourselves away as Jesus did? It is not as simple or clear-cut as that, of course, yet if we see ourselves as our brother's or sister's "keeper," we will not consider it a failure when we give away our good things for their care and benefit. If we do not believe that we belong to each other, we will hold on as tightly as we can, until what we have left is too much of a burden to be a gift. Both Abel and Cain brought their first fruits as an offering to God. The statutes and ordinances for sacrifices in the Old Testament all require first fruits and animals without blemish. God gave his first and only child Jesus to humanity, the one we believe was without sin, to show us abundant mercy and love. This is who we are, people who are thankful and generous *before* we have nothing left of value to give.

My favorite Bible story (Matt. 15:22–28) deserves repeating. Even Jesus needs to be convinced that his caregiving is for all, not just the children of Israel. The Canaanite woman, who changes Jesus's mind about healing her daughter, asserts that they are not dogs but also children of God, and therefore worthy of all Jesus has to give. That does not erase what he has already said about them, but even Jesus can choose to change his stance. His healing of that Canaanite daughter foreshadows sharing the Good News with the Gentiles, which includes most Christians today. There are other scriptures that also widen Jesus's embrace. Jesus says "I have other sheep that do not belong to this fold" (John 10:16), which means we do not know all those whom he considers his family. He also laments that some of those whom he loves refuse to be gathered in: "How often have I desired to gather your children together as a hen gathers her brood under her wings, and you were not willing!" (Matt. 23:37). Any idea we have of who Jesus considers his people is likely too narrow.

From Family Picture to Big Picture

Mothering begins with small, largely unnoticed actions, adding up over time. Grassroots organizing does too. We build trust over time by listening to each other's stories, sifting out what will be strong enough to weave a person's commitment into the movement for the long haul. Mothers especially have extensive practice at unheralded behind-the-scenes support, which is what organizing efforts need.

It is my first job as a mother to keep my children's bodies safe. Just as God is described by the psalmist, "You hem me in, behind and before, lay your hand upon me" (Ps. 139:5), my joy over the little one learning to crawl, walk, and run was paired with child gates, special locks on some cabinets, protection on sharp corners, and instructions about things that cannot be climbed or played with. I could protect them as long as I had childproofed their environment or was there and watching. Putting them on the school bus raised my levels of both pride and terror; after all, we live in a time when elementary-aged children have "active shooter" drills at school.

Bathing, clothing, feeding, and holding my children's bodies are the physical ways I testify to them every day that their bodies matter. Black, brown, and indigenous mothers and fathers do the same for their children. Yet people with black or brown bodies are shot by police much quicker and at drastically higher rates than white people; black and indigenous girls are trafficked at much higher rates. Where is the public outcry? The solidarity of motherhood and love for our children must compel not only people of color but white people to demand justice for all our children. In the interviews with many black mothers and activists for her 2019 book *We Live for the We: The Politics of Black Motherhood*, author Dani McClain tells stories of balancing motherhood and activism, time spent with our own children and time away in order to bring systemic change for everybody's children. She articulates the real fears she has as an African American mother protecting her own daughter from: discrimination at school, objectifying in public, and maybe even someday receiving prejudiced maternal health care. There is a tension there that is shamefully absent among white America.

After the protection of my children's bodies, my greatest drive is to protect the expansion of their minds, to give them hope, echoing God's words in Jeremiah, "For surely I know the plans I have for you, says the Lord, plans for your welfare and not for harm, to give you a future with hope" (Jer. 29:11). My daughters' imaginations should have the freedom to grow, thinking about who they will become and what beauty is and does. Beauty and creativity are not a limited resource—I will fight for the right of every child to dream, especially for girls to go to school so their dreams are an actual possibility. It is definitely a risk to the status quo in traditional cultures, to be open to education and more possibilities for girls and women. I am compelled to advocate for children in refugee camps or detained at the southern border of the United States receiving books and instruction too. All children's minds and imaginations must be free to dream.

We are better versions of ourselves when we are in awe, more faithful to the image of God in us. Wonder and appreciation of any kind of art improve our mental health and renew our spirits. Mothers and other intimate caregivers plant the seeds of wonder and awe when we point out to our children spider webs sparkling with dew or laugh together at a loud, colorful clown. We "consider the lilies of the field" together (Matt. 6:28). We are our children's first sensory cues for pleasure, as anyone who has seen a child's face light up when they see their mother or hear her can attest.

If you search for words such as "beauty" or "songs" in the Bible, half the references seem to be positive, praising God, while the other half describe being mocked or scorned by people. That is what human beings do to beautiful things we do not understand. We stand in awe, then turn around and objectify or mock them. I want my children and all children to be able to surrender themselves to awe and wonder in the presence of beautiful things, ideas, and creativity. How do we advocate for that? The church has a long history of sacred art. We need to be willing to commission and fund artists who pull back the veil on the beauty of God in our time, even if their art is not in familiar styles. (There are so many options to replace a painting of a fair-haired, blue-eyed Jesus.) When it inspires a sense of our own value and proportion in the face of an awe-inspiring God, it is advocacy to support such art. The Carnival de Resistance visited our metro area a few years ago, and art as advocacy came alive for my family. It was weird, in a wonderful way. We played carnival games to knock down the forces of empire and witnessed musical and theater performances that testified to faith-led dismantling of colonial power. The volunteers in residence in the "village" for that time ate common meals from foods gleaned or donated, conserving power and other resources while putting most of their time into building relationships. The entire project, which has repeated in different cities, is a testimony that art changes the perspective and commitments of those who engage with it.

When our child is affected, mothers will protest in the streets. The mother of one of my middle school classmates adamantly insisted on mainstreaming kids with disabilities into regular classrooms, because her daughter with cerebral palsy deserved to receive her education among peers. Congresswoman Lucy McBath became a gun control advocate and successfully ran for office after her son Jordan Davis was shot and killed by a white man at a gas station. Congregations may be moved to start ministries with people who have developmental disabilities when the pastor has a child with Down syndrome. I know several that have taken the step of attaining our denomination's "open and affirming" designation after their pastor's child came out as LGBTQ. Does it have to be this way with every single injustice? Do we have to have a specific face and name, perhaps the pastor's own child, to move our congregation into action? We have that personal connection through Jesus, if we are willing to recognize his solidarity with all people who are scorned, oppressed, traumatized, and disabled.

Mothers and other caregivers know that ultimately we need to be preparing our children not for independence, but for loving interdependence with others: siblings, friends, perhaps even a spouse. Similarly, pastors work to nurture ecumenical, interfaith, or global companion relationships, connecting our congregations to others so we can learn to care about the things the other cares about. Jesus connected people who thought they had nothing to do with each other, and the Advocate, the Holy Spirit, carries on the work through us. What if we viewed the famous John 3:16 passage with an emphasis on God so loving the "world" instead of focusing on our own sense of who may be included in "whosoever believes in me"?

QUESTIONS FOR REFLECTION

Clergy Women:

1. When has love for your child motivated a congregation to act?
2. What experiences have widened your own motivation to be your brother's or sister's "keeper" across different demographics?
3. Reflect on a time when you addressed discrimination or injustice as a congregation. What worked well, theologically or practically? What would you do differently?

Support Network:

1. If you were to describe your congregation from the perspective of abundance, what would you say? What are the resources you have access to, which you could share with others?
2. What do you read, to whom do you listen, and how do you vet your sources to learn about motherhood and faith from others?

ACKNOWLEDGMENTS

〜

This book would not exist without my dual vocations as mother and pastor. Yet neither would it have come to fruition without the space to step away from both of those demanding roles in order to write. I am incredibly grateful to my husband Stefan, for believing in my abilities and the way the Holy Spirit works through my writing. My children Vikta and Greta, and the ways we change each other, were my strongest motivation to recognize God's own mothering behaviors. I am thankful for my own mother, who loves church more than anyone I know, and taught me how to be a mother. My entire family's encouragement strengthened my own persistence in finding a way to bring this crucial conversation to a wider audience through this book.

I am particularly grateful to the communities of clergy women that continue to shape my ministry and outlook, especially Young Clergy Women International (and now its alumnae) and the online group for Lutheran Leader Moms. The feedback of colleagues from these groups and my personal network has shaped the content and made it absolutely clear to me that writing this book is part of my calling. Thank you especially to Pastor Jen Hackbarth who asked me to become her writing partner, and during the course of our monthly meetups my earlier book proposals evolved into this essential one. I have hope for the future witness to the gospel of Jesus Christ in the world because of the mothering leaders I am honored to call friends. I acknowledged already, but let me do so again, that the theology of a mothering God is accessible to me because I benefit from the legacy of women clergy and feminist theologians who laid the groundwork years before I ever considered seminary. I am grateful for my deeply thoughtful editor Nancy Bryan and the staff at Church Publishing Incorporated who have supported this book.

SUGGESTED READING

Women in Ministry

Andy Kort and Mihee Kim-Kort, *Yoked: Stories of a Clergy Couple in Marriage, Family, and Ministry*, 2014.

Karoline Lewis, *SHE: 5 Keys to Unlock the Power of Women in Ministry*, 2016.

Ashley-Anne Masters and Stacy Smith, *Bless Her Heart: Life as a Young Clergy Woman*, 2011.

Allison M. Moore, *Clergy Moms: A Survival Guide to Balancing Family and Congregation,* 2008.

Martha Spong (ed.), *There's a Woman in the Pulpit: Christian Clergywomen Share Their Hard Days, Holy Moments and the Healing Power of Humor*, 2015.

Family Metaphors for God

Claire Bischoff, Elizabeth O'Donnell Gandolfo and Annie Hardison-Moody (eds.), *Parenting as Spiritual Practice and Source for Theology: Mothering Matters*, 2017.

Sarah Jobe, *Creating with God: The Holy Confusing Blessedness of Pregnancy*, 2011.

Kelley Nikondeha, *Adopted: The Sacrament of Belonging in a Fractured World*, 2017.

Lauren Winner, *Wearing God: Clothing, Laughter, Fire, and Other Overlooked Ways of Meeting God*, 2018.

Activism

Cynthia Wang Brandt, *Parenting Forward*, 2019.

Alexis Pauline Gumbs, China Martens and Mai'a Williams (eds.), *Revolutionary Mothering: Love on the Front Lines*, 2016.

Jennifer Harvey, *Raising White Kids: Bringing Up Children in a Racially Unjust America*, 2017.

Dani McClain, *We Live for the We: The Politics of Black Motherhood*, 2019.

Related blogposts and article links can be found on the author's website: leeannpomrenke.com